Aleksandŭr Stamboliĭski

Makers
of the
Modern
World

Aleksandŭr Stamboliĭski
Bulgaria
R J Crampton

HH
HAUS HISTORIES

First published in Great Britain in 2009 by
Haus Publishing Ltd
70 Cadogan Place
London SW1X 9AH
www.hauspublishing.com

A CIP catalogue record for this book
is available from the British Library

ISBN 978-1-905791-77-4

Series design by Susan Buchanan
Typeset in Sabon by MacGuru Ltd
Printed in Dubai by Oriental Press
Maps by Martin Lubikowski, ML Design, London

Contents

To
Richard Langhorne,
The Most Generous of Friends

Preface

There were virtually no negotiations in Paris in 1919 as far as Bulgaria was concerned; the victorious Allies dictated a peace settlement. As with all surviving states, however, the settlement of 1919 was a pivotal point in that state's historical evolution and this book sets out to explain the factors leading to and the consequences flowing from that pivotal point.

In 1919 the Bulgarian state was but 41 years old and to many of its citizens it must have seemed like a state with a great future behind it. From the inception of the state to 1913 a new political entity had emerged. It had not produced the perfect democratic system but it was far from being an autocratic one. Its economy was developing and it had proved its military strength in a short war against Serbia in 1885 and in the First Balkan War of 1912 when, in conjunction with the other Balkan states, it destroyed the Ottoman Empire in Europe. Most of the territory gained in the latter conflict was lost following the terrible gamble which precipitated the Second Balkan War of 1913. Bulgaria's desire to undo the consequences of that war led it to align with Germany in both the great conflicts of the 20th century. Yet many Bulgarians would argue that Bulgaria's travails began not with the gamble of 1913 but when the Great Powers, primarily Britain and Austria-Hungary, destroyed the large Bulgaria created at San Stefano and replaced it with the virtual rump state devised by the Treaty of Berlin. This author, as a Briton, has been subjected to more than one tongue-lashing by irate Bulgarians fulminating at the injustices of Berlin. It is to be hoped that the entry of Bulgaria into the European Union in January 2007 will finally still such passions.

The man who dominates the following text, Aleksandŭr Stamboliĭski, fulminated more at internal than external injustices. He was to lead a movement of extraordinary interest and originality. Agrarianism in general and Bulgarian agrarianism in particular have scarcely received the historical attention they merit. For Bulgarian nationalist historians it has always been the external questions which have dominated their writings and when the communists came to power Stamboliĭski and his agrarians were shunted onto a branch line which led to nowhere whilst the main route was taken over by the disciples of Marx and Lenin who alone understood the true laws of history. And communist historians were also far from free of the nationalist instincts which had so disapproved of Stamboliĭski's radical ideas on that front.

The intention of this book is to concentrate on the years from 1878 to the late 1940s. These were the years when Bulgaria was overwhelmingly a society of small peasants, and they were years dominated by the ideas and actions of Stamboliĭski. He was born the year after the foundation of the modern state and although he was murdered when only 44 years old his ideas were retained and cherished by the peasants who formed the majority of the population. The agrarian movement remained of great potential, and at times actual strength until the second half of the 1940s. It was the consolidation of communist power which destroyed agrarianism and Stamboliĭski's legacy; the communists decapitated agrarianism by removing its political leaders and then destroyed its social basis through the collectivisation of agriculture.

Writing on the history of East European societies presents the author with a number of methodological inconveniences. Most of the area is ethnically mixed and the differences in language mean that geographical features have a variety of names. I have used the ones most familiar to the English reader or the ones which seem to me the most historically appropriate; hence Constantinople is preferred to Istanbul, at least until the end of the First World War. Dates, too, present problems. The Orthodox Church retains the Julian calendar and so did most states in which that church was dominant. Bulgaria did not adopt the Gregorian (Western) calendar until April 1916. Until that date I have used the Julian version which in the 19th century was 12 and in the 20th century 13 days behind the Western calendar. Transliteration from the Cyrillic script generates considerable controversy amongst experts; I have risked my neck by using a system of my own. It is set out on p x.

In the many years that I have been a student of Bulgarian history many colleagues in Bulgaria, Britain and elsewhere have given help and inspiration, as have the students it has been my privilege to teach in Oxford and to examine there and elsewhere. They are too numerous to mention individually but I am always conscious of my collective debt to them. An individual debt too great to quantify is that to my wife who has been the most important part of my life for even longer than Bulgarian history has been the focus of my work.

Transliteration Scheme

а	a		ф	f
б	b		х	h, but 'kh' in Russian and Ukrainian words
в	v			
г	g (always hard)		ц	ts
д	d		ч	ch
е	e		ш	sh
ж	zh, but д/ж as 'dj'		щ	sht, but 'shch' in Russian and Ukrainian words
з	z			
и	i			
й	ĭ		ъ	ŭ
к	k		ь	not transliterated at the end of words, but 'y' when used in conjunction with 'o'
л	l			
м	m			
н	n			
о	o		ю	yu
п	p		я	ya
р	r			
с	s			
т	t		The Russian letter, 'ы' is transliterated as 'y'.	
у	u			

List of Abbreviations

ACC	Allied Control Commission
BANU	The Bulgarian Agrarian National Union
BANU-NP	The Bulgarian Agrarian National Union-Nikola Petkov
BCP	Bulgarian Communist Party
BWP	Bulgarian Workers' Party
CLS	Compulsory Labour Service
DSR	Directorate for Social Renewal
FF	Fatherland Front
GNA	Grand National Assembly
IMRO	Internal Macedonian Revolutionary Organisation
NSM	National Social Movement
PR	proportional representation
SDP	Social Democratic Party

King 'Foxy' Ferdinand of Bulgaria with Dimitŭr Stanciov, his Bulgarian tutor and future advisor to the Bulgarian delegation in Paris.

I
The Life and the Land

1
The Emergence of Modern Bulgaria

The Bulgarians were an amalgamation of the Turkic Bulgars who crossed southwards over the Danube in the 7th century and the resident Slavs whom they subjugated. The Bulgars were pagan and the Slavs Christian and the amalgamation did not begin until after the Bulgar ruler had enforced Christianity upon all his subjects in the late 9th century. The new religion also brought literacy and literature. A critical question was whether the Bulgarian Church should align with Rome and the West or with Constantinople (modern Istanbul) and the East. Bulgaria's ruler decided that the Church should adhere to the east and thus the Bulgarian Church acquired the doctrine, the liturgy and the customs, political as well as religious, of the Orthodox Church.

Though Bulgaria shared its religion with its mighty neighbour, the Byzantine Empire based in Constantinople, there was frequent political tension between the two states. The Bulgarian ruler, Simeon the Great (r. 893–927), twice brought his armies to the walls of the imperial capital. His prowess was such that he became the only ruler, apart from the Emperor himself and the Holy Roman Emperor, whom the Byzantines

Turkey, Greece and Bulgaria 1912–1923

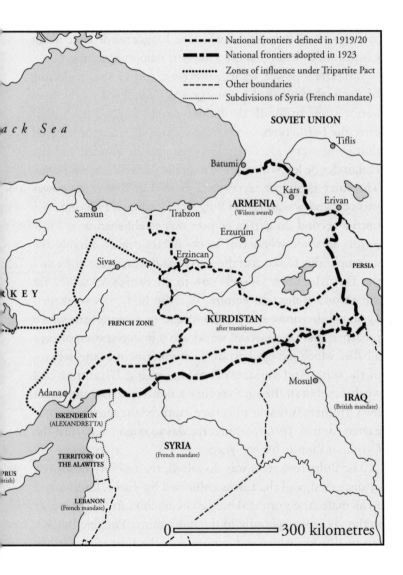

National frontiers defined in 1919/20
National frontiers adopted in 1923
Zones of influence under Tripartite Pact
Other boundaries
Subdivisions of Syria (French mandate)

ack Sea

SOVIET UNION

Tiflis

Batumi

Kars

Erivan

ARMENIA
(Wilson award)

Samsun

Trabzon

Erzurúm

Sivas

Erzincan

PERSIA

RKEY

FRENCH ZONE

KURDISTAN
after transition

Mosul

Adana

IRAQ
(British mandate)

ISKENDERUN
(ALEXANDRETTA)

SYRIA
(French mandate)

TERRITORY OF
THE ALAWITES

PRUS
itish)

LEBANON
(French mandate)

0   300 kilometres

5

recognised as a 'Basileus' or King. More importantly, he secured the independence of the Bulgarian Church which was given its own Patriarch and which no longer needed to consult Constantinople on major ecclesiastical appointments.

Bulgaria's power waned, however, and at the beginning of the 12th century the country was conquered by the Byzantine emperor, Basil 'the Bulgar-slayer'. Legend has it that after the battle of Belassitsa the victorious emperor ordered that 99 in every 100 Bulgarian prisoners be blinded and the remainder be left with one eye to guide their colleagues home. The story is almost certainly a myth[1] but Byzantine power was real and was to last in Bulgaria for almost two centuries until a second Bulgarian empire was established in 1185. It produced some wonderful works of arts, most notably the incomparable frescoes in the church at Boyana near Sofia and the Tsar Alexander Gospels now in the British Museum. Yet the second Bulgarian empire, like the first, was weakened by social divisions and by the spread of bogomilism which preached that the material world was a manifestation of evil, a belief which did not encourage commitment to the defence of the state. And the state needed defending. Byzantium had weakened but in the 14th century a new force had appeared: the Ottoman Turks. In 1393 they captured the mediaeval Bulgarian capital, Tŭrnovo. Bulgaria was to remain a part of the Ottoman Empire for 500 years.

The Bulgarian state was dissolved, the nobility destroyed or dispersed, and the towns colonised by Turks, Greeks and Armenians, their original Bulgarian inhabitants taking refuge in the villages, especially in the mountains. The one Bulgarian institution which did survive was the Bulgarian Orthodox Church. It was the Church which kept alive the written language and Bulgarian folk traditions, many of which were interwoven with Christian festivals; even Bulgarian names survived primarily because Church christenings continued.

There were few signs of a Bulgarian national revival until the second quarter of the 19th century, and when the revival movement did appear – the Bulgarians call it the *vŭzrazhdane* or 'renaissance' – it was primarily cultural rather than social or political. It expressed itself initially through the Church. The Bulgarian Patriarchate which had survived the conquest of 1393 was suppressed in 1767 and placed under the control of the Oecumenical Patriarchate in Constantinople, an organisation dominated entirely by Greeks. Bulgarian bishops were rapidly replaced by Greek ones. In addition to being Greek the Oecumenical Patriarchate was also corrupt with clerical office being sold to the highest bidder. By the late 18th century Bulgarians began to complain because their bishops were corrupt; by the 1820s they there were complaining because their bishops were corrupt and Greek; by the 1840s they were complaining because their bishops were Greek.

Education was controlled by the Church and therefore also fell under Greek cultural domination. In the 1830s and 1840s the Bulgarians launched a drive to increase education. In the circumstances the educational reformers wanted education which was more secular and less dominated by Greek language and culture. By the second half of the 19th century the drive to educate Bulgarians, in Bulgarian, had made remarkable progress.

In addition to establishing a network of schools the Bulgarians also had to provide the books for use in teaching, the presses on which to print them, and, not least, a standard language in which they were to be written. That these were found was another testimony to the energy of the national renaissance.

EDUCATION IN BULGARIA
The first secular school in Bulgaria was opened in Gabrovo in 1835. It was funded partly by Bulgarians in Russia and used the mutual method of instruction because there were too few qualified teachers. In 1840 it was reorganised into classes. Greek was still taught in many Bulgarian schools but in most the majority of subjects were taught in Bulgarian. Some of the early schools were co-educational but in 1841 the first girls' school was founded in Sliven. By 1878 over 2,000 schools had been established, 150 of which were for girls. The funding for the schools came in part from Bulgarian communities abroad, especially in Russia and Romania, but also from the guilds which flourished with the growth of manufacturing and trading in Bulgaria. The guilds also funded a large number of Bulgarian students who went abroad for the higher education their homeland could not offer. The majority of Bulgarians educated abroad went to Constantinople or to central and western Europe, many of them funded by scholarships; in 1867 the city of Plovdiv alone was financing five students in Paris, four in Vienna, seven in Russia, two in Britain, and 40 in Constantinople. The scholarships were necessary as most students were from poor backgrounds. The education movement was one of the most important elements in the alliance between the peasants, the guilds and the intelligentsia, an alliance which was the bedrock of the national revival. So important was education to the Bulgarians of the Tulcha diocese in the Dobrudja that the local Bulgarian council decided that villages should be allowed to have only one tavern, the revenue from which was to be used to finance local schools. After 1878 the Bulgarian state provided free and compulsory primary education. Secondary schools were fewer in number but many of them, especially in Macedonia, were of a high standard.

The pupils who attended these schools, or who were sent on scholarships in institutions of higher learning outside the Bulgarian lands, were not drawn from a social or a political elite. Since the destruction of the Bulgarian nobility Bulgaria had been largely an egalitarian society and those who graduated from the new schools were overwhelmingly the children of ordinary peasants or townsfolk. The newly emerging educated cadres, or intelligentsia, were therefore drawn directly from and initially at least remained close to the peasant mass of the nation.

There was little social differentiation in the rural communities but divisions were beginning to appear in the towns. In the second and third quarters of the 19th century a new wealthy Bulgarian mercantile and manufacturing element emerged, much of it based on selling uniforms to the Ottoman army. Given this economic nexus this new element may not have wanted political disturbances but it was fully behind the cultural revival, and it provided much of the money which funded the schools, and the many scholarships provided to study in them or abroad.

Most of the manufacturers and merchants were organised into guilds which financed the schools and also the rebuilding of many churches and monasteries. It was the Church, rather than the educational movement, which lay at the heart of the Bulgarian national revival, whose chief demand was for an independent Bulgarian Church, separate from the Constantinople Patriarchate. Success was eventually achieved in 1870 when the Ottoman government accepted that a separate Bulgarian Church, headed by an Exarch, a rank inferior to that of Patriarch, should be established. The Patriarchate, however, refused to recognise the new institution which it declared schismatic in 1872. No matter what pressure the Bulgarians exercised the Greek Patriarchate remained immovable on this point. The schism did not end until 1945.

It was in part frustration at the stalemate in the Church struggle which gave increased credibility to the small number of Bulgarians who had been calling for political as well as ecclesiastical independence. A few armed bands had been formed and had crossed from Serbia or Romania into the Bulgarians lands in the late 1860s but they had been defeated. In the early 1870s a network of potential insurgents was established in Bulgaria, the chief organiser of these being Vasil Levski. Levski was betrayed and executed in 1873 but two years later enough of his organisation remained to take advantage of the Ottoman Empire's difficulties in the Balkans, difficulties caused by a tax revolt in Bosnia in 1875 and by a war with Serbia in 1876.

In April 1876 the revolutionary organisation issued a call to arms. Few responded and they were soon contained, but the suppression of the revolt occasioned a series of outrages against innocent civilians, most notably the murder of around 5,000, mostly women and children, in Batak and Peshtera. The massacres aroused the anger of Europe; Gladstone raged at them and in Russia the Pan-Slavs demanded action to save the Bulgarians from further suffering. That action came first in the form of a diplomatic initiative intended to force the Ottomans to introduce reforms but the guarantees for the implementation of these reforms were considered insufficient in St Petersburg. In June 1877 Russia declared war on the Ottoman Empire and sent its armies into the Balkans. By February 1878 the Russians had almost reached Constantinople and at San Stefano dictated a peace settlement which created a huge new Bulgarian state stretching from the Aegean to the Danube and from the Black Sea to the mountains of western Macedonia.

Britain and Austria-Hungary feared that the new state would be a massive wedge of Russian influence in the Balkans and they therefore insisted upon a revision of the San Stefano settlement. That revision took place in July 1878 and the resultant Treaty of Berlin reduced the new Bulgarian state to a rump territory between the Danube and the Balkan mountains. The area between the Balkan and the Rhodope mountains was to be an autonomous province of the Ottoman Empire, Eastern Rumelia; northern Dobrudja was to be given to Romania; and the Morava valley was to go to Serbia, whilst the remaining territories of Macedonia and Thrace were to be returned to the Sultan's rule with nothing more for their comfort than a promise that the administration of the area would be reformed.

It could be argued that Bulgarian nationalism, as a mass popular force, was more the consequence than the cause of political liberation. The rising of 1876 had not received widespread backing but the losses inflicted by the Treaty of Berlin aroused massive popular resentment. Some of the wrongs of Berlin were to be rectified in 1885 but the pain at the loss of Macedonia was to remain as bitter and powerful a force amongst Bulgarians as the loss of Alsace-Lorraine was for the French.

ooooo

The new, truncated Bulgaria was to be a principality but a vassal state of the Sultan, which meant it could not establish full diplomatic or even commercial relations with most other states. It was also to be a constitutional monarchy, with its monarch to be chosen by the Great Powers. Their choice was the German princeling, Alexander of Battenberg.

The young prince arrived in his new principality after a constituent assembly at Tŭrnovo had drawn up a liberal constitution which shared power equally between the prince and the unicameral legislature, the 'sŭbranie' or assembly. By a decision of the Russian Provisional Authority which governed Bulgaria before the Tŭrnovo system came into operation, the capital of the new state was to be the small garrison town of Sofia. It was chosen primarily because it was the crossing point of the north-east to south-west and north-west to south-east routes across the Balkans. It was also near the new border with Ottoman Macedonia.

The delicate political balance between prince and parliament proved difficult to maintain and in 1881 Alexander suspended the constitution and imposed his own authoritarian rule. It did not work. He could not carry the main political forces with him and in 1883 the Tŭrnovo system was restored.

Born in Verona in April 1857 Alexander Battenberg was a much-liked nephew of the Tsar of Russia and a favourite of Queen Victoria. The prince fought in the Russian army during the Russo-Turkish War of 1877–8, a fact which naturally increased his prestige in both Russia and Bulgaria. After Alexander left Bulgaria he joined the Austro-Hungarian army and married an actress with whom he had two children. He died in Graz in 1893 aged 36. By his own wish his body was buried in Sofia. His mausoleum was closed by the communists in 1947 but was refurbished and re-opened in 1991.

Two years later Bulgarian nationalists in Eastern Rumelia carried out their own coup and declared for union with Bulgaria. The prince could scarcely resist a move so welcome to his subjects and he travelled to the Rumelian capital, Plovdiv, in triumph. At the same time he moved most of his small army to the south to counter any retaliation by the Ottomans. The latter accepted the union but so rapid an increase in Bulgaria's size aroused great suspicion in Serbia. With the Bulgarian army concentrated in the south without any rail link to the principality, the Serbian king decided to act and invaded Bulgaria. In an astonishing national effort, and one in which ethnic Turks as well as Bulgarians took part, the Bulgarian army marched, most of the time literally, to meet the advancing Serbs. In November the decisive battle was fought at Slivnitsa, some 30 miles from Sofia. The Serbs were repulsed and had it not been for Austro-Hungarian diplomatic intervention the Bulgarian army could have taken Belgrade. In February 1886 the Treaty of Bucharest restored the *status quo ante*; Bulgaria made no territorial gains at the expense of Serbia and its presence in Eastern Rumelia was accepted only in that the prince of Bulgaria was recognised as the governor-general of the province.

This revealed a deep fissure in Bulgarian political affairs which not even the achievements of 1885 could mend. Alexander's name had not been mentioned in the treaty because the Russians did not want to see his position strengthened; if he had been named even as governor-general of Eastern Rumelia it would have been more difficult to remove him. And his removal was what the Russians now desired.

Alexander had angered the Russians in a number of ways. He had refused to allow them to establish virtual control over the Bulgarian National Bank and had been equally resistant to their efforts to determine the shape of railway development in the principality. Alexander had also tried, unsuccessfully, to bring German officers into the Bulgarian army to supplant the Russians who, up to 1885, supplied all officers above the rank of major. (That these officers had been recalled to Russia before the Serbo-Bulgarian war of 1885 made Bulgaria's military victory even more astounding.) But most important of all Alexander had embarrassed the Russians. By the mid-1880s Russian foreign policy was concentrated upon expanding Russian influence in Central Asia and St Petersburg did not want to have to divert its attention from there to the Balkans where stability was what was now required. The Russians were therefore enraged at what they believed had been Alexander's failure to warn them of the forthcoming union with Rumelia, a not entirely justified interpretation of events. They were also disturbed because in 1885 the Bulgarian authorities had not prevented exiled Macedonians calling for action to force the Porte, the Ottoman government, to implement the promised reforms for Macedonia. Even worse from the Russian point of view was that some Macedonians and their supporters had taken matters into their own hands and had financed armed incursions from Bulgaria into Ottoman Macedonia. Such action could precipitate chaos in the Balkans and was therefore greatly feared by Russia.

For his part Alexander had much to complain of in Russian conduct. Russia's military officers and their diplomatic representatives frequently behaved in an arrogant and overbearing fashion. They seemed to believe that because their armed forces had liberated the country they should be given preferential treatment within it, be it in the granting of contracts or in the determination of where railway lines should be built. They also believed that Bulgaria should follow the Russian line in international affairs, a view shared by a number of prominent Bulgarian politicians.

The Russians encouraged these and other critics of Alexander and hinted that they would not object to his removal. This took place in a military coup in the summer of 1886. But supporters of Alexander neutralised the putschists and invited the prince to return. The Russians were saved when Alexander announced that he would return to Bulgaria if the Tsar of All the Russias, whose armies had in effect given him his throne, approved of his return. A relieved Tsar Alexander III said he did not approve and Alexander retired to Vienna.

It was not until the summer of 1887 that a new prince, Ferdinand of Saxe-Coburg-Gotha, was found; he was to become known as 'Foxy' Ferdinand. The Russians refused to recognise him and until they did no other power would do so. Bulgaria was in effect an international pariah. Virtual international isolation was accompanied by threats from Russia and by conspiracies which, if not sponsored by Russian officials, certainly included some renegade Russian activists. Ferdinand's defence against these machinations lay in the hands of his prime minister, Stefan Stambolov.

Stambolov had risen to prominence in the Bulgarian Liberal Party and from 1887 to 1894 he devoted his energies to keeping Ferdinand on the Bulgarian throne. This meant taking tough action against the prince's enemies and imposing rigid controls on the political machinery of the country. He also managed to secure concessions for the Bulgarian Church in Macedonia which brought him great popularity within the country.

The means Stambolov used to secure Ferdinand on the throne were sometimes extreme and the Bulgarian political system suffered for many years as a result of this, not least in that it alienated many of the peasantry who, on the one hand, could not understand why Bulgaria should be at odds with Russia but on the other could see that whatever political views they might have would not make any difference to those who ruled them. Political apathy therefore increased and a widening gap appeared between the peasants and the political establishment.

Stambolov succeeded in keeping Ferdinand on his throne

Born the son of an innkeeper in Türnovo in 1854, Stefan Stambolov was educated there and at a seminary in Russia. He was expelled because of his connections with Russian revolutionaries. He joined the nationalist activists in Bulgaria and proved his ability as an organiser. After the liberation he was elected speaker of the parliament even though legally too young for that post. After his departure from office he became the victim of Macedonian extremists. In July 1895 he was attacked in one of Sofia's main thoroughfares. His assailants hacked off his hands. Three days later Stambolov died.

but he failed to secure any concessions from Russia with regard to recognition. By 1894 Ferdinand had concluded that Stambolov had served his purpose and he was engineered out of office. Recognition of Ferdinand by Russia followed two years later, but the main reason for it was not the removal of the former prime minister but the fact that Ferdinand agreed that his son Boris, born in 1894, be received into the Orthodox Church which the Bulgarian constitution demanded and which Ferdinand's spiritual master, the Pope, had forbidden.

Ever since the Treaty of Berlin, but even more so after the union of 1885 had liquidated the Rumelian problem, Macedonia had played a vital role in Bulgarian affairs. It had fuelled Russian anger over Alexander's conduct. By securing concessions for the Bulgarian Exarchate in Macedonia Stambolov had repaired the breach with the Bulgarian Church caused when Ferdinand, shortly after his arrival, had flaunted his Catholicism, but by reigning in the Macedonian activists lest they give Russia cause for direct intervention in Bulgaria, Stambolov had earned their undying enmity. Stambolov had based his Macedonian policy on the precepts that Bulgaria was in no position to impose its own solution in the area, and that Russia would prevent it from joining with other Balkan states to solve the question themselves. The only alternative was to cooperate with the Porte to secure concessions for the Bulgarian cause; this policy, argued Stambolov, should be easy to implement because the Porte, facing disorders in Armenia, would cooperate in order to secure stability in the Balkans, to which the Russians also should have no objection.

The price of cooperation with Constantinople was one which was too high for some Bulgarian nationalists. They wanted Bulgarian power established in Macedonia and were prepared to resort to arms to secure it. By the late 1890s a powerful organisation, the Supreme Committee, had emerged in Sofia. It sought to promote armed intervention in Macedonia, the object being to precipitate such disorder that the powers would intervene, as had happened in Bulgaria after the April Uprising in 1876. But by the late 1890s there was another organisation, known to history as the Internal Macedonian Revolutionary Organisation (IMRO). Its objective was autonomy for Macedonia, and an autonomy which was not to be, as it had been in Eastern Rumelia, a prelude to incorporation into Bulgaria, but an autonomy which would be preserved when Macedonia became, along with the existing Balkan states, an integral part of a Balkan federation.

IMRO was not the only new factor in the increasingly complex Macedonian question. In 1897 a dispute over Crete had brought about a war between Greece and the Ottoman Empire, a war in which the Greeks were rapidly and soundly thrashed. This ended fears that the Ottoman Empire, 'the sick man of Europe', was about to expire. Furthermore, the Greeks now turned their attention away from Crete and towards Macedonia where they began to back efforts by the Greek Patriarchists to check or reverse the advances made amongst the local Christians by the Bulgarian Exarchate. With the Bulgarians and Greeks increasing their cultural offensive the Serbs were determined

Reliable statistics on the ethnic composition of Macedonia before the First World War are impossible to obtain. The Greeks counted all Orthodox Christians as Greeks. The Bulgarians regarded language as the better measure for ethnicity and insisted that the Slavs of Macedonia spoke Bulgarian. The Serbs believed that Macedonia was 'Old Serbia' and that its Slav inhabitants spoke a Serb dialect. Many of the inhabitants were neither Christian nor Slav. The other groups included Turks, Jews, Roma, and Albanians, and the religious diversity was almost as bewildering; there were even ethnically Jewish Muslims. Hence the culinary macédoine of vegetables.

not to be left out and the Serbian Orthodox Church also initiated campaigns to win over the Macedonian Christians to their side.

Greek and Serbian efforts to win over the local Macedonians increased after 1903. In August of that year there was a widespread uprising in Macedonia and parts of Thrace. There was huge popular support for the rising in Bulgaria but the country's rulers dared not defy Russia and intervene. The hapless rebels were left to their unenviable fate. Thousands fled to exile in Bulgaria; for many of those who remained in Macedonia the stark choice lay between starvation or alignment with the Greek or Serbian Church.

The suppression of the 1903 rising was a setback from which the Bulgarian cause in Macedonia never fully recovered, but that did not prevent Macedonia remaining at the centre of Bulgarian foreign policy for another 30 years. By 1903, however, many Bulgarians were worried less about Macedonia than about their own immediate future.

2
Bulgarian Society and the Birth of the BANU

At liberation four-fifths of the population of Bulgaria and Eastern Rumelia were rural dwellers and the proportion in 1920 was little different; even in 1946 it was still above three-quarters. Of the rural population almost all were peasant farmers, the vast majority of them with holdings of under 10 hectares.

They were not all Bulgarian. The long centuries of Ottoman rule had brought about significant changes in the ethnic composition of the Bulgarian lands. Much of the rich agricultural areas had been colonised by Turks, and Greeks had become dominant in some of the larger towns, particularly south of the Balkan mountains. During the upheavals of 1876–8 many Turks left but despite their exodus almost a quarter of the population (702,000 out of 2,814,000) at the beginning of the 1880s consisted of ethnic Turks; the Greeks made up 1.5 per cent and the Bulgarians 67.84 per cent. By the end of the century there had been a further fall in the Turkish population. In absolute numbers there were 540,000 in 1900 which represented 14.41 per cent of the total; by 1920 the proportion had fallen to 11.20

MINORITIES IN BULGARIA

Bulgaria's record for the treatment of minorities is generally an impressive one. Anti-Semitic outbursts were uncommon and Bulgarians understandably take pride in the fact that the Jews of Bulgaria proper survived the Second World War. Relations with the Greek minority were good until events in Macedonia drove a wedge between the two communities in the 1900s. A treaty of 1919 provided for a population exchange between Bulgaria and Greece. Others who found refuge in Bulgaria were Armenians, sailors from the battleship *Potemkin*, and thousands of White Russian refugees.

The decline in the number of Turks after 1878 had a number of causes. The main one was that they could not accommodate themselves to the ethos of a Christian-dominated society. They disliked the greater freedom enjoyed by women, they suspected compulsory education was biased against Islam, and they feared conscription, though many Turkish soldiers displayed great valour in the war of 1885. In Rumelia the land tax forced many to emigrate because levies had previously been on produce; now fallow land, which featured largely in Muslim agriculture, was also taxed. At times legislation gave unintentional offence, as when the Rumelian authorities banned the cultivation of rice because the paddy fields were breeding grounds for malaria-bearing mosquitoes, but rice was the staple food of the Muslims who saw the restriction as an attack upon the Islamic way of life. In the early 1920s Bulgaria was more tolerant of traditional Islam than was Atatürk's Turkey, but the 1930s saw the introduction of policies aimed at homogenising Bulgaria to produce a Christian, Slav society. These failed, as did policies with similar objectives imposed by the ailing communist regime of the 1980s. The latter produced the largest ever egress of ethnic Turks, over 300,000 of whom left Bulgaria, though around a third later returned. After 1989 the Movement for Rights and Freedom attracted its support from the Turkish minority which formed around 10 per cent of the population.

per cent. The emigration of Muslim landowners from Bulgaria and Rumelia had important social consequences, not the least significant of which was that land was available and therefore these areas avoided the land hunger which gripped other parts of Europe such as Ireland or southern Russia.

The result was that Bulgaria became, even more so than

before, the land of the small peasant proprietor. The large estates which had existed in Bulgaria before 1878 were mostly Muslim-owned and were to be found predominantly in the Maritsa valley. Many of these estates had not been farmed as a unit but had been rented out to small producers but there were some holdings which had been worked commercially and most of these were now also broken up and distributed as small units. After the mid-1880s large, commercial farms in Bulgaria were to be found mostly in the rich arable region of the southern Dobrudja in the extreme north-east of the country.

The small peasant proprietor, either as a renter or owner of the property concerned, had been the dominant feature of the Bulgarian rural landscape for generations; it was because most peasants had land that social demands were seldom raised by Bulgarians in the 19th century. In many communities peasants could provide almost all they needed from their own resources; one report spoke of a peasant building a house and needing to purchase outside his village only roof tiles, nails and window frames. In most communities land was held not in compact holdings but in strips distributed throughout the village's three or four large fields. The practice of allowing all sons – and at the end of the 19th century all daughters – to inherit land meant that the division of properties was later to become a problem. Regulation of the agricultural year was the responsibility of a village council of elders which would sometimes decide not only when sowing, harvesting etc, should take place but also what crops were to be grown. The main crop was cereals which accounted for approximately three-quarters of agricultural production in the late 1890s and fodder crops which were a further 18 per cent. Peasants grew their own vegetables and vines but often these were on separate strips outside the main fields and in many cases in different villages, frequently because those strips had been acquired as part of a marriage settlement. Crops cultivated for industry were rare, though south of Kazanlŭk was the famous Valley of the Roses where the flowers were grown for distillation into valuable rose oil, most of which was exported.

Animal husbandry played an important role in the life of the Bulgarian peasant. After the mid-1820s wool was in great demand for the merchants and manufacturers who were supplying the cloth for the uniforms worn by the Ottoman army. Most villages kept communal flocks of sheep and individual peasant households would have poultry, a pig or two, and perhaps a draught animal; in the south the latter would often be water buffalo. Large flocks of sheep were reared commercially and often driven long distances to summer or winter grazing. Some were driven on the hoof to the markets of the large towns such as Adrianople (Edirne) and Constantinople (Istanbul). There was movement of people as well as animals. Thousands of Bulgarians, usually organised into gangs, went to work as market gardeners or agricultural labourers in Turkey, Romania, Serbia, Hungary or even as far as afield as Austria.

Life for most Bulgarian peasants, at least until the end of the 1890s, was frugal but secure. Inevitably, the emergence of the new Bulgaria precipitated changes, not all of them beneficial to the established way of life. Transhumance, for example, which had been so important in the rearing of sheep, was made more difficult by the new national frontiers established after 1878. The policies of the new state also demanded adaptations by the peasants. Modernisation inevitably comes at a social price.

The new Bulgaria wished to make itself a modern state.

Its constitution had decreed that there should be universal primary education and that all males would be conscripted for a period into the new Bulgarian army. By the mid-1880s a national plan for railway construction had been enacted and plans had been set in motion to build modern port facilities at Varna and Burgas on the Black Sea. In the mid-1890s the government of Konstantin Stoilov, who succeeded Stambolov, launched a national programme for the promotion of Bulgarian industry.

This new infrastructure had to be paid for. In the principality of Bulgaria in 1879 government expenditure had been the equivalent of 39.75 million leva; in 1897 it was 95.29 million leva and the union of Bulgaria and Rumelia did not account alone for this increase. In the early 1880s the Bulgarian minister of finance, Petko Karavelov, had stated that peasants paid with least displeasure those taxes with which they were familiar and, this being so, he intended to continue to rely on the traditional Ottoman sources of revenue: stamp duty on all documents from passports to fishing licences, fines, excise duty on salt and other necessities, the tobacco monopoly, and above all the tithe on agricultural produce.

The tithe had many disadvantages. It was levied by village and the harvest could not be taken in until the tithe had been assessed, a stipulation which often led to crops spoiling in the fields. The crop, when harvested, had to be taken to official collection points, a wearisome and lengthy process which was carried out at the peasants' expense. The assessment of the tithe value frequently occasioned corruption by officials. Nor was the tithe an efficient source of revenue for the government. The delays in taking in the harvest which it caused meant that Bulgarian produce frequently missed the early market opportunities in central Europe which the country's southerly position should have created. More importantly, Bulgaria's main crop was cereals and the last quarter of the 19th century was the worst of times to have to rely on this as the main item of national income. Grain was being produced so cheaply in North America that by the 1880s Canadian or US produce was sold more cheaply on the Hamburg exchange than crops from East Prussia. And production from Australia and Argentina was soon to make the competition even tougher and, with the introduction of refrigerated shipping, to cheapen meat and fruit products.

So inadequate and cumbersome was the tithe that it was abolished in Rumelia immediately after 1878 and replaced by the tax on land so disliked by the Turks. In 1882 the principality also did away with the tithe but it replaced it not with a land tax but with a cash levy equivalent to recent tithe values. This was a burden for many peasants because the years chosen to assess the cash value were ones in which prices had been high. They were now considerably lower and so as peasant revenue from his crops decreased the tax levied on it increased. By the mid-1880s many families could no longer meet their tax obligations and some six million leva of cash levies remained uncollected. After the political upheavals of 1885–7 Stambolov decided to revert to payment in kind, and this decision also applied to the former Eastern Rumelia. There was little rejoicing in the villages and when grain prices took another nosedive in the early 1890s the government revenues also fell. In 1892 cash payments were restored but this time with an assessment process more favourable to the peasant. The revenue produced, however, was no greater and in 1894 the modernising Stoilov administration scrapped the system altogether and replaced it with a land tax.

For the Bulgarian peasant it seemed that government would

impose whatever form of levy was least advantageous to the producer. There were further reasons for growing peasant resentment at the tax system. It was unequally levied between town and country, with the towns paying much less per capita; a study in the Varna region in 1895 revealed that peasants there paid six times more than members of the free professions and 20 times more than a government official. Furthermore, the burden on the peasant was increasing at a faster rate than that on the urban dweller. If the peasant tax burden for the years 1878–83 is taken as an index of 100, the index for 1889–92 was 154. Stoilov had stated that his modernisation schemes were intended to make Bulgaria 'the Belgium of the Balkans'. The Bulgarian peasant would have welcomed complete success in this endeavour; in 1892 a Belgian citizen paid 6.5 per cent of his income in tax but a Bulgarian peasant was required to hand over 12.5 per cent of his.

By the 1890s another problem was increasingly affecting the Bulgarian countryside. With the exodus of Muslim landowners after the liberation of 1878 a great deal of land had been available for purchase. Many Bulgarian peasants seized the opportunity to increase their holdings. They had, however, little capital of their own. Nor could they borrow easily from state or other concerns. Before 1878 there had been a network of Agricultural Savings Banks, established by a reforming Ottoman official in the 1860s. During the war of 1877–8 many of the banks had been destroyed and their documents burned or dispersed; and after 1877 many of their former borrowers had fled or now refused to pay interest on their loans with the result that, although the Agricultural Savings Banks began to amass capital again in the late 1880s, they still lacked the funds to finance wide scale new purchases. Nor could banks founded after the liberation take their place. In 1893 the state-owned Bulgarian National Bank had only five branches and three agencies outside Sofia, and except in that city, Plovdiv, Varna and Rusé commercial banks hardly existed. In the early 1890s another source of capital appeared in the form of agricultural cooperatives. The first was founded in 1890 in Mirkovo in the Pirdop district. In future years the cooperatives were to become an essential feature of Bulgarian peasant life and were to be close to the political movement which undertook to defend and promote the interests of the peasantry.

In the meantime, before the cooperatives had established themselves the Bulgarian peasant looking for money to purchase land and the means to work it had to turn to the private money-lender. There was little effective control of usury and interest rates were extremely high. Many peasants fell victim to the process whereby they would pay off some of their debt obligations by selling all or part of their crop to the usurer whilst it was still unharvested. The price for this 'on the stalk' crop was set by the usurer and was invariably well below market values, often forcing the peasant to borrow again later in the year. In some cases the peasant's only escape from indebtedness was to sell his land to the usurer and either emigrate to the town or rent his former property from its new owner. In many cases he had no option but to do so; in 1902 Stamboliĭski noted, *It is no uncommon occurrence for the wretched debtor not only to be left without the means to sustain himself but to be thrown into the street like a cast-off rag and for his family to be left to the mercy of fate.*[1]

The plight of the peasants did not escape the attention of some sections of the Bulgarian intelligentsia which feared that a new gulf was opening up to divide it from its former allies. A number of Bulgarian authors and activists, most notably Todor Vlaĭkov, adopted attitudes similar to those of the Populists in Russia and in the 1890s there were attempts to form village associations to defend the peasants against exploitation. A powerful advocate of such action was Yanko Zabunov who in 1896 was appointed director of the state vinicultural institute in Pleven. Zabunov's words and those of his fellow advocates of peasant mobilisation did not fall on deaf ears; in the years 1896–9 150 local peasant organisations were established. But in the three months between October and December 1899 around 100 were established.

The reason was that in October 1899 the government, hard pressed to finance a disastrous railway construction project, decided that for the years 1900 to 1905 the land tax would be replaced by a tithe in kind. There was widespread anger and protest at the announcement. Many peasants and their supporters in the intelligentsia – teachers, priests, agricultural advisors and vets – seized upon an idea floated in January 1899 by Tsanko Tserkovski that the peasants should set up an organisation similar to a trade union which would promote their interests; he ruled out a political party, not least because he feared it would compete with the Bulgarian Workers' Social Democratic Party of which he was a member. In April a meeting near Tŭrnovo endorsed Tserkovski's idea and called for an agrarian congress to convene in Pleven in December. In an apt reflection of the peasant-intelligentsia alliance it was to meet after Christmas when there would be little work to do in the fields and when the teachers would be on holiday.

The congress attracted 845 delegates, most of them peasants, from 45 out of Bulgaria's 71 administrative districts, though the majority of the delegates came from the northeast where protests at the tithe in kind were most intense. The congress set up the Bulgarian Agrarian Union and elected an eight-man central governing council, which included Tserkovski. The new organisation was avowedly not a political party and, according to its temporary statues, its purpose was 'to raise the intellectual and moral standing of the peasant and to improve agriculture in all its branches'. There were also calls for specific reforms to achieve this end, these including commassation or the consolidation of separate strips into compact holdings, measures to provide cheap credit to farmers, and steps to find markets for agricultural produce. But the most strident demand was for an immediate end to the tithe in kind.

The first objective was to urge the national parliament to reject the government's proposal but this was not achieved, the sŭbranie enacting the requisite legislation in January 1900. After this disappointment the Union concentrated on sending petitions to Prince Ferdinand and on holding protest meetings, some of which were extremely large by Bulgarian standards. The monarch, however, would not listen and in March announced he would receive no more supplications on the question of the tithe. This only intensified peasant anger and subsequent protests became more violent with the meetings now demanding a limitation of Ferdinand's power as well as the end of the tithe in kind. The most serious confrontation took place on 19 May in the village of Darankulak in the Dobrudja when between 120 and 150 people were killed and over 800 wounded; not all the victims were protesters. Thereafter the agitation declined, not least because the busiest time of the agricultural year was approaching, but enough peasant anger remained to ensure that in the local elections held in August 120 local councils passed into the control of pro-Agrarian Union activists, the peasants having been urged by the Union to vote for candidates who pledged themselves to support an agrarian programme.

A second congress was held in December 1900 in which the governing council was doubled and a three-member permanent council was established. The second congress also called for education to be tailored more to the needs of agriculture and for greater legal security for the peasant landowner, including the right to a minimum area which was to be inalienable even in the case of bankruptcy. The second congress reiterated the Union's insistence that it was a pressure group rather than a political movement: 'We do not seek power, we shall form no ministry', it stated. But this was a line that was increasingly difficult to hold.

To demand, as the Union did, that the tithe in kind be rescinded was in essence a political demand; the insistence that the prince's growing personal power be limited was an overt political statement. The delegates to the first two congresses were united in their detestation of the existing political parties but experience was to show that it was only political organisations which could win political victories in the political arena.

Despite reiterating the view that the Union was a non-political body the second congress had also urged that in the elections which were to be held in February 1901 peasants should vote for specifically agrarian candidates. They did with the result that 23 agrarians were elected to the sŭbranie. This encouraged those in the Union who wanted to transform it into a political organisation. So too did the sequel to the elections. Of the 23 new agrarian deputies seven immediately defected to the established parties, being enticed to do so by offers of jobs or contracts. When the third congress met in Sofia in October 1901 Tserkovski and his allies were on the defensive as the majority of the delegates were now convinced that if agrarian deputies were not to be suborned by the established parties the Union would have to transform itself into a political organisation and conduct its own political campaigns. This view prevailed. Tserkovski was voted off the permanent council and the organisation was renamed the Bulgarian Agrarian National Union (BANU). Its objectives were now to bring about the regeneration of 'the peasantry and the entire nation'.

In 1900 Stoilov had recognised that the established political parties had lost the support of the vast majority of the nation whose true defenders were the agrarians who, he believed, were now the strongest political force in the land. The third congress seemed to confirm that view. The leadership reported, probably with some exaggeration, that the organisation now had almost 800 local branches or *druzhbi* (friendly associations) and over 35,000 members.

The strength perceived by Stoilov, however, was potential rather than real. When the BANU's fourth congress met in Shumen in October 1902 the leadership reported that of the 400 *druzhbi* established during the tithe struggle only 40 remained, and at the fifth congress in Stara Zagora in the following year the picture was even worse. The handful of delegates who turned up were told that almost all the *druzhbi* had disappeared and that the finances of the party newspaper were in so parlous a state that it could appear only irregularly. Furthermore, in the elections of 1903 not a single BANU candidate had been returned. This was in part because the victors at the election, the Stambolovist party, used tough measures against their opponents. The BANU had also been weakened by the divisions in its leadership over the question of making it a political body, and the temporary departure of the defeated Tserkovski and his colleagues had removed a sizeable part of the established leadership cadres. There were by 1903 also signs of an improvement in conditions in the countryside, an important cause of this improvement being the development of cooperative credit facilities.

By 1908 the BANU's position had been reversed once again and in elections that year the force of Stoilov's analysis became clear. One of the most important reasons for this reversal in BANU's fortunes was the appearance of a dynamic new leader.

3
The Rise of Aleksandŭr Stamboliĭski

The BANU had been wiped clean from the sŭbranie plate in 1903. It was demoralised and almost bankrupt. Yet in the elections of May 1908 the Union attracted over 100,000 votes, 11.2 per cent of the total, and had 23 deputies in the new assembly; the agrarians were the largest of the non-government parties in the sŭbranie. In local elections held later in the year the party secured control of almost 300 local councils. At the tenth congress in Sofia in November it was recorded that there were now 1,123 local party *druzhbi*.

This remarkable turnaround was in part a result of the poor harvest of 1907 which had sharpened the peasants' political consciousness and when the peasants did begin 'to think politics' they looked to the BANU. The Union had introduced a number of benefits to help peasants, including a life insurance scheme for members of the local *druzhbi*. It had also introduced a National Store in whose local branches peasants could purchase, at reasonable prices, agricultural equipment and other products. Even more importantly, the Union had played a pivotal role in expanding the cooperative movement. In 1906 and 1907 the Union was also responsible for founding 81 reading rooms, or *chitalishte*, but much more important were the BANU's activities in stimulating the cooperative movement and above all the cooperative credit system. The Union and the cooperatives, together with their associated banks, were always to be closely linked, and the advances made by the credit cooperatives were one of the most important reasons for the improvement in rural living conditions which took place between the turn of the century and the First World War.

The *chitalishte* originated in Serbia. The first Bulgarian *chitalishta* was opened in Silistra in 1856 and the institution spread rapidly both inside the Bulgarians lands and amongst Bulgarian communities in exile. They were primarily intended as places to read (the word means 'a place for reading') and would stock newspapers, periodicals and books in Bulgarian and other languages. They also provided a place for amateur dramatics, adult literacy classes and meetings; a number were the venue for secret assemblies of revolutionaries. They still exist.

Another reason for the BANU's electoral success in 1908 was that it had carried out a series of internal structural reforms. These had streamlined its organisation and had brought its headquarters to Sofia. They had also greatly increased party discipline. These reforms would have been less effective if the party had not at the same time evolved a new and coherent political ideology directed firmly towards the interests of the peasantry. It was one of the most original political doctrines to appear in Europe in the early 20th century. It was very much the work, as were the structural reforms, of Aleksandŭr Stamboliĭski.

ooooo

Aleksandŭr Stamboliĭski was born in the southern Bulgarian village of Slavovitsa in March 1879. His surname was acquired because his father had made a number of visits to

Constantinople or 'Stambul' in Turkish. The Stamboliĭski family was neither rich nor poor; their life was, like most of their fellow peasants, hard but not impossible. Stamboliĭski's mother died soon after his birth and his father remarried. The new mistress of the household already had two children and she had little affection for her stepson. Stamboliĭski attended the local village school where his natural abilities were soon noted, but his hopes of continuing his education were opposed by his father and stepmother who wanted him to work on the family land. The strong-minded Stamboliĭski refused and left home to study in the secondary school in the nearby town of Ihtiman. Upon graduation from there in 1893 he won a place at the state agricultural school in Sadovo. It was here that he first indulged in political activities, his participation in a student demonstration leading to his dismissal from the school in 1895.

From Sadovo Stamboliĭski moved to the state vinicultural institute in Pleven where he remained until 1897. Here he became close friends with Yanko Zabunov who took the significant step of making Stamboliĭski an editorial assistant on the journal *Oralo* (derived from the verb 'to plough'); it was in journalism that Stamboliĭski was to make his name. In 1898 he became a teacher in a village near Slavovitsa. His attended the Pleven congress in 1899 but he made little impact there; he was young and the tithe issue was not a burning one in his native area. He did, however, reconnect with journalism and in May 1900 published his first article in the agrarian newspaper, *Zemedelsko zashtita* (Agrarian defence). In the autumn of the same year Stamboliĭski wrote longer pieces in which he argued that the Bulgarian state was failing to make real economic and social progress and was wasting money by aping foreign, western institutions, a coded reference to the monarchy, and by building up a large army and civil service.

For the next two years personal rather than public affairs dominated Stamboliĭski's life. In the summer of 1900 he had married a fellow teacher, Milena Daskalova. In September 1901, he and his wife moved to Halle in Germany where Stamboliĭski had enrolled in the university. He did not stay long. Having contracted TB in February 1902 he was forced to return to Bulgaria. He moved to a small mountain village where he made a complete recovery.

Soon after his recovery he re-engaged in the agrarian movement, and once again made his main impact in journalism. In a series of articles between 1903 and 1908 he worked out the main ideology of the movement and refined its political tactics and its organisation. By 1907 his energy, ability and dedication had made him one of the top three or four agrarians and by 1910 he was generally acknowledged as the movement's leading figure. In 1908 he had been elected to the sŭbranie. His energy was noted by one who

> 'A barrel-chested farmer who possessed a rare ability to translate sharp rural wit into the language of political struggle.'
> MISHA GLENNY[1]

observed him closely in the early 1920s: 'Stamboliĭski was the essence of his race. He had all the qualities of a Bulgarian, and not quite all his faults. Huge in stature, broad in proportion, big-shouldered, uncouth in his movements and vehement in speech, he impressed everyone with his energy, his sincerity and his fearlessness. His big brown face was topped with a shock of black hair, and his upturned moustaches helped to give his appearance a certain fierceness. There was a combative twinkle in his eyes, a deep furrow in the forehead between them, and a nose not without fineness.

His frankness was refreshing in a country where it is the rarest of qualities. Not that he was wholly devoid of a peasant's cunning; or free from the thriftiness of his class and the avidity of his race.'[2]

Another observer recalled him as a man '... of medium height and thick-set build, and he has black, curly, ruffled hair, deep-set eyes and a prominent chin, which give to his expression the force, character and energy for which he is renowned. One feels, too, whilst he is obviously a peasant, possessed of little learning and knowing no language except his own, that M. Stambolisky is gifted with a power of observation and a capacity for acquiring information which are rare in such men, and that from every standpoint he is a "live wire"... he strikes one as a personage who is honest, frank and open ...'[3]

Stamboliĭski never lost, nor sought to lose, the outward appearances of his peasant origins. He spent as much time as he could on his own holding and took considerable, and apparently justified pride in the quality of the wine he produced. His earthiness did not exclude enjoyment of a lewd joke whatever the company and at times his conduct was that of the peasant. Nadezhda Stanciov, who served as his advisor and interpreter during and after the Paris Peace Conference, described how 'she could hear Stamboliiski in the room next to hers rattling his wash basin and spitting into his handkerchief and then the next day sit down to breakfast with him when he appeared "very neat, shaved, red, gay, making jokes on love."'[4] She thought him astonishing, not least because of the disparity between his humble background and his intelligence and ability. No doubt he was also a man of ambition who could at times be overbearing but he nevertheless earned and retained the respect and admiration not only of the BANU's mass following but also of the great majority of his close colleagues.

Stamboliĭski enjoyed the company of women to whom he was attractive. He also, when in Sofia, paid frequent visits to the theatre. These visits had to be curtailed after February 1923 when a bomb was thrown at him in the auditorium. It was an ill omen.

ooooo

Between 1903 and 1908 Stamboliĭski had pioneered the reconstruction of the BANU. He had abandoned his early view that the Union should not engage in direct political activity and had been instrumental in drawing up the 1905 'Code for the Participation of the Bulgarian Agrarian National Union in Legislative Elections'. It regulated the selection of agrarian candidates and, with the experience of the 1901 elections in mind, greatly increased the discipline which the party, as it may now be described, exercised over those who stood as its local or national representatives. To prevent political jobbery it was decreed that no one could stand as a BANU candidate unless they had been a member of the Union for at least two years, a period which was extended to five years in 1911. The effectiveness of the reforms was seen as soon as the sŭbranie elected in 1908 convened. The agrarian deputies were no longer easy prey to the jackals of the old parties. They were now a disciplined and coherent body which held rigidly to the platform on which it had been elected; as Stamboliĭski wrote, *A social organisation which wishes to live and wants to be fit for combat must have iron discipline …*[5]

Other important changes in the BANU were enacted at the ninth congress in November 1907. The organisation's headquarters were then in the southern Bulgarian town of Stara Zagora where its titular leader, Dimitŭr Dragiev, lived. Since the foundation of the Union it had been argued that a provincial headquarters would keep agrarianism separate from Sofia and the venality associated with the capital and the political establishment. As the movement gradually increased in strength this view became less tenable. Sofia may have contained venal politicians but it also contained banks, communication facilities and journalists. If the BANU was to follow a political course its distance from the national centre would be a disadvantage. Stamboliĭski pressed for a move to Sofia and, despite the opposition of Dragiev, carried the day. Stamboliĭski also persuaded the ninth congress to reform the leadership of the Union. The existing three-man standing committee was replaced by a larger one in which Stamboliĭski was the dominant figure.

The BANU had become a political party but Stamboliĭski and his associates insisted that it was not a political party of the old type. They were still regarded as useless lackeys of the palace, as mere factions *ready to sell out, to abase themselves for a mess of pottage, for the sake of office ...*[6] In 1904 Stamboliĭski had asserted that the old parties were *parasites on the body of the nation – they have to die; they will die: and the sooner the better.*[7] And when it was reported that an incoming party was negotiating with its predecessor in office, Stamboliĭski likened the conversations to *the whisperings of two robbers on the steps of a house full of goodies, one of whom is leaving with a sack full of swag while the other is getting ready to go in with the same aim – plunder.*[8] The agrarians were different, Stamboliĭski argued, in composition, capability, morals, internal structure, means, objectives, methods, principles and programmes, activities, and the exercise of power.[9]

These reforms were important in strengthening the BANU's electoral and political strength, but the organisation would not have progressed as far as it did without a simultaneous refining of its ideology. For this Stamboliĭski was again largely responsible. His ideas were expressed in the many articles he wrote in the agrarian press and were condensed in *Political Parties or Estate Organisations?* published in 1909; in 1919 he further refined and developed his thinking in *The Principles of the Bulgarian Agrarian National Union.*

Stamboliĭski's ideology differed considerably from that of the other radical political movement of the day, socialism. Stamboliĭski did not see private property as an evil but accepted it as the motive force for work which gave men satisfaction and a sense of purpose and dignity. Stamboliĭski believed that there were two aspects to human nature, the individual and the communal. Private property satisfied the demands of the former but, he argued, as society developed individuals would realise that in this more complex environment the welfare of the individual depended increasingly on the well-being of the whole; thus a communal consciousness would develop. This would lead to a system in which communities worked together for the common good but in which the constituent families would continue to own their property: work would be collective but ownership would remain private. A communal consciousness would not tolerate any individual having too much or too little property; egalitarianism was thus an inevitable result of communal consciousness. For this reason the agrarian movement called for the redistribution of property, taking land from the Church, the crown and the state and handing it to the landless and to those who did not have enough to support themselves and their families.

From these ideas derived the concept of 'labour property', or the ownership of the means of production by those who worked them. Work, not ownership, was the determining factor in the way society was divided which meant that Stamboliĭski rejected the socialist notion that society was divided into mutually antagonistic classes defined by the relationship of the individual to the means of production. Rather society consisted of 'estates' which were defined by activity. Those engaged in the same occupation had common economic interests even though they might be of differing social origins; thus a small peasant farmer working his land was of the same estate as the rich peasant or even the large landowner who did the same; even tenant and landlord could be of the same estate. In Stamboliĭski's analysis society consisted of seven estates – agrarian, artisanal, wage-earning, entrepreneurial, commercial and bureaucratic – though he did not exclude the possibility that other estates might emerge as society developed yet further.

By far the most important of these estates was the agrarian. This was not merely because it was numerically the largest and produced the essentials of life; it was also because it allowed the individual the greatest scope for development and self-fulfilment. And it was in the village that man had real and direct contact with the natural world on which he ultimately depended. Stamboliĭski always regarded the village as the best of human communities and was later to do much to improve conditions in them. His dislike and distrust of the towns was increased by the fact that in them were concentrated those who were holding back the economic development of the peasant and the country: the bureaucracy, the royal family, the army and the lawyers. The latter figured prominently in the agrarians' list of demons.

These ideas underlay the BANU's political programme. This called for the redistribution of land, especially from the Church, and the imposition of a maximum limit for individual land holdings. It also demanded much greater spending on agrarian issues which included more rural education, mass insurance schemes and better public health provision. The agrarians also wanted the abolition of government monopolies on the sale of salt, matches and other necessities. A major item in the programme was for a complete ban on private usury and for more help for the cooperative movement and its banks; the cooperatives were also to be encouraged to build storage facilities for harvested crops. It was through the cooperatives, Stamboliĭski argued, that a communal consciousness could most easily be developed.

The BANU also put forward a number of political demands. It wanted the election of all public officials, the repeal of recent anti-trade union legislation and the end of what it called police terror, to be followed by the implementation of full civil liberties for all Bulgarian citizens. Female suffrage was another demand, as was that for proportional representation (PR) and the granting of full regional and local autonomy. The agrarian programme was a costly one but the BANU countered any criticism on this score by saying it could be paid for by the introduction of a progressive income tax and by massive reductions in expenditure on the bureaucracy, the legal profession, and above all on the monarchy and the army.

Stamboliĭski and his followers were overt republicans, not least because of Ferdinand's attitude to the tithe protesters in 1900. But they did not call for the immediate establishment of a republic. In 1911 Stamboliĭski quipped that if Bulgaria had been a republic from 1878 all the failings of the system would be laid at its door *and we would now need to have a huge royalist, monarchist party*. As the continuation of his speech showed, the agrarians were pragmatic republicans: *In our view the notion of a republican government is not a matter of principle but of tactics. When we in our agrarian associations want the election of councillors, deputies, ministers, teachers, judges and so on, we can not but also want the election of the head of state, but when that wish becomes reality will be determined by circumstances.*[10] Not that Stamboliĭski pulled his punches when dealing with monarchs: *Five centuries of savage and bloodthirsty Turkish rule has left its legacy deep in the soul of all Bulgarians and has conjured up a hatred for crowned heads, for autocracy and for monarchism. And, for their part the princes who have happened to alight upon the Bulgarian throne, have done everything possible to increase, reinforce and entrench this popular hatred.*[11]

There was little peasant opposition to this view, but the proposed reduction in military expenditure was more controversial. It was undeniable that the army absorbed up to a third of the national budget, and that borrowing to purchase military equipment had weakened the country, but the army was still seen by many as the only means by which national reunification could be achieved. The BANU's answer to that was simple. National reunification would not come about by the clash of arms. It would be achieved by social and political evolution and by cooperation. As the individual developed a communal consciousness so separate states would develop an international consciousness, particularly if they rid themselves of royal/military cliques and moved to agrarian rule. International consciousness would bring about voluntary associations which would culminate in the formation of federations. One of these would be a Balkan federation in which all the Bulgarian lands would be included. The national question would be solved by international cooperation.

There was not to be time for this evolution to occur. Shortly after the BANU's electoral triumph of 1908 agrarian republicanism and internationalism were to have to cope with aggressive monarchism and intensified popular, traditional nationalism.

4

The Years of War (1912–18)

When the national assembly met after the elections of May 1908 the BANU deputies immediately bared their teeth against their monarch; they refused to applaud his speech from the throne and in the following session Stamboliĭski launched a vehement attack upon the prince. It was the opening skirmish of a long and bitter battle. The next round was fought in the autumn.

The vassal status which the Treaty of Berlin had imposed on Bulgaria was proving increasingly irksome in the 1900s, not least because it limited Bulgaria's freedom of action in matters such as the setting of tariffs. In September 1908 Ferdinand pronounced Bulgaria a fully independent state and declared that he was no longer the Prince of Bulgaria and governor-general of Eastern Rumelia but 'King of the Bulgarians'. Ferdinand was working in tandem with Austria-Hungary which also revised the Treaty of Berlin by annexing Bosnia and Hercegovina which it had administered since 1878. This angered Russia until brusque diplomatic intervention by Germany resolved the crisis; the Russians then engineered a financial settlement which compensated Turkey.

At the domestic level Ferdinand's declaration was not universally popular. The russophiles disliked the fact that independence had been secured through cooperation with Austria-Hungary, Russia's competitor in the Balkans. The Macedonians feared that the declaration might mean that Ferdinand and his government had accepted the territorial situation in the peninsula as permanent, though these anxieties were to some extent assuaged by Ferdinand's taking the title of 'King of the Bulgarians' rather than 'King of Bulgaria'.

There was another cause for concern amongst many politicians, amongst whom the agrarians were prominent. Ever since the fall of Stambolov in 1894 Ferdinand had increased his personal influence and power to such a degree that he had imposed a 'personal regime'. This was based on his control of ministerial appointments, a control facilitated by *partisanstvo*, the Bulgarian version of clientism and corruption which meant that sŭbranie votes could be bought via contracts and jobs; it was routine for most state and local government officials to be changed when a new government was formed in Sofia. Furthermore, elections, with the exception of those in 1901, were held not to determine what form of government the nation wanted but to ensure a workable parliamentary majority for an administration already chosen by Ferdinand. And when the prince decided that he wished to change his government he could easily destabilise it, often by having recourse to the extensive files he kept on all active politicians. The personal regime meant that Ferdinand could dominate Bulgarian affairs whatever national opinion might be.

The declaration of independence in 1908 was seen by many as an example of Ferdinand's personal rule. The agrarians refused to accept the new title of 'Tsar' (King) and continued to refer to Ferdinand as prince. In his speech to parliament

Stamboliĭski said that the declaration had not brought independence to Bulgaria but had underlined the country's *servile position under the rule of the personal regime, and it has placed the country in a more shameful position than even the most backward African province ... since its foreign policy and financial affairs have been turned over to Russia and Turkey.*[1]

Stamboliĭski feared that Ferdinand's personal rule was backed by the military. The agrarian leader therefore denounced the cost of the army and also pointed out that the purchase of military equipment from abroad offered rich pickings to corrupt politicians and merchants. But Stamboliĭski's concerns went deeper. He feared the officer corps might separate itself from society and, with the monarch, put itself above the law. Stamboliĭski and the BANU were not the only critics of the personal regime. The National Party, led by Ivan Geshov for whom Ferdinand entertained a visceral hatred, was extremely critical, though less intemperate than Stamboliĭski.

In March 1911 the workings of the personal regime were seen when Ferdinand decided that the administration of Aleksandŭr Malinov's Democratic Party, which had come to office in 1903, had served its purpose. That administration had introduced a number of reforms, including the use of referenda in some questions of local government and the first, limited experiment in PR. Malinov's government was replaced by a cabinet headed by Geshov and dominated by the National Party.

The intense personal antipathies between king and prime minister were overcome for reasons of foreign policy. Malinov had based his on the hope that cooperation with Constantinople would bring concessions for Bulgaria. It did not work.

The Serbian Church was given an important Macedonian bishopric and Malinov failed to secure the right to construct the coveted rail link between Bulgaria and Macedonia. (Agreement to build the link, from Kyustendil to Kumanovo, was not reached until the 1990s.) If Bulgaria's interests were to be advanced in the Balkans it would have to be by other means. Bulgaria was too weak to attempt action on its own and therefore if action were to be taken it would have to be with others. No great power would align with Bulgaria and therefore the solution had to be that Bulgaria act in consort with the other Balkan states. The Serbs, however, would not work with Malinov because of his joint action with Austria-Hungary in 1908; if progress were to be made in Belgrade Malinov would have to be replaced and Bulgaria would have to swing round to a more pro-Russian and less pro-Austrian position. But before any real progress could be made towards a new diplomatic alignment between the Balkan states constitutional reform had to be enacted to accommodate the 1908 changes in Ferdinand's title.

The constitution of 1879 stated that constitutional revision had to be carried out by a Grand National Assembly (GNA), a parliament twice as large as the ordinary sŭbranie. The GNA to endorse the changes in Ferdinand's title met in June 1911. It produced another fierce clash between the monarch and the BANU which had 55 deputies in the assembly. Stamboliĭski argued that Ferdinand had no right to open the GNA until it had decided whether or not to accept the change in his title and therefore when the monarch began to speak Stamboliĭski rose to do the same. His protests were quickly brushed aside and Ferdinand's new title endorsed, but there was much greater questioning of proposed changes to Article 17 of the constitution on which there was a ten-day debate.

The original proposal was to give the king the power to negotiate and conclude treaties with foreign states, the argument being that in the Balkans the situation was so complicated that there was an absolute need for secrecy. The amendment was rejected and it was decided that these powers should rest with the government, but, again because of the need for secrecy, the government was to inform the sŭbranie only 'if the interests and security of the state allow it'. Given Ferdinand's domination of foreign policy and the stranglehold he could exercise over ministers there was little doubt that if the king wanted secrecy he would get it. The changes in Article 17 further entrenched Ferdinand's personal regime.

The National Party government attempted to counteract this by extending PR to cover the entire country. This would be introduced when the next elections were held and, the Nationalists believed, would make it more difficult to manufacture a majority for a newly-appointed administration. Ferdinand's view was that it would lead to even greater fragmentation in the political parties which would make it easier for him to play one off against another.

For the immediate future, however, the main preoccupation of monarch and government was foreign affairs. The Bulgarian position in Macedonia was weakening. Serbian bishops were appointed to two more sees and increasing instability in the territory had led to the deaths of a number of Bulgarians. There were further disorders in the spring of 1912 which enflamed public opinion in Bulgaria; by the summer the country was seething with war fever and demands for government action.

In fact the government had done much behind the scenes. Since the summer of 1911 Geshov had been negotiating with the Serbs. Initially his approaches had been rebuffed because he called for the traditional Bulgarian solution to the Macedonian problem: autonomy. The Serbs knew that this, as in Rumelia, was intended to be the prelude to incorporation into Bulgaria and therefore insisted upon partition. This Geshov had to accept and lines were drawn, but between the acknowledged Serbian and Bulgarian portions there was to be a 'contested zone' whose fate was to be determined by further negotiations or, should these prove fruitless, by the arbitration of the Russian emperor. On this basis a secret political agreement was signed in February 1912 which was followed by an equally secret military convention in April. Political and military accords were concluded with Greece in May and September, though these contained no provisions for the division of conquered territory. Verbal agreements were reached between Montenegro and the other states in the summer of 1912. The Balkan league was complete.

Stamboliĭski had never been an advocate of war. Despite increasing popular demand for action he wrote in September 1912: *We cannot possibly want war with Turkey because we know what terrible consequences it will bring for our people who work on the land, who will fill the barracks, and whose children will be sacrificed on the field of battle; we cannot possibly want war because we do not know, and we have no way of knowing, under what conditions we will find ourselves, whether Bulgaria will be in a fit state diplomatically, financially and militarily to fight a war; we cannot want war because we do not want to bear the responsibility for such an adventure.*[2] Stamboliĭski's voice went unheeded. King and cabinet had decided upon war in August and in October, to general popular acclaim, the long-expected conflict began.

If the war was not unexpected the course it took was. The Ottoman army was still highly regarded after its victories over

Greece in 1897 but by November a series of massive defeats had confined it to Salonica, Ioanina, Adrianople and the defensive complex at Chatalja which guarded the Ottoman capital. Ferdinand had dreams of entering Constantinople and even ordered a set of sumptuous robes for the occasion. Geshov, more pragmatically, thought an occupation of Constantinople would give Bulgaria immense strength in the forthcoming peace negotiations. It was not to be. An attack on the Chatalja lines, ordered by Ferdinand against the advice of his generals, failed, and soon thereafter the exhausted Bulgarian troops were attacked by an enemy far deadlier than the Turks: cholera.

After the assault on the Chatalja lines Bulgaria's fortunes declined. Peace talks began in London but a change of government in Constantinople brought a less conciliatory administration to power. It refused to surrender Adrianople and in February fighting resumed. Shortly thereafter Romania demanded compensation for the increases in territory which the other Balkan states were going to secure. The only area where that could be found was in the southern Dobrudja. Meanwhile, in London, talks between the Balkan allies and the Turks made little progress until the British foreign secretary, Sir Edward Grey, cut the Gordian knot and told the delegates to sign or leave. They signed.

The Treaty of London defined the boundaries between the victorious Balkan states and what was left of the Ottoman Empire in Europe, and it insisted that a new Albanian state be created in the west of the peninsula. But it did not regulate the boundaries between the existing Balkan states.

Bulgaria had hoped to secure the majority of Macedonia and argued that the conquered lands should be divided in proportion to the military involvement and sacrifice of each state. Greece and Serbia wanted the final settlement to produce a balance in the Balkans which would ensure peace in the future. There were two main bones of contention: Salonica and the contested zone. The Bulgarians and Greeks had raced towards Salonica, the Bulgarians losing by no more than a few hours. With Serbia no agreement could be found on the contested zone and the Tsar of Russia was therefore asked to arbitrate. But when this request was made the Bulgarians demanded that the judgement be delivered within eight days.

The Russians were enraged. As a great power they were not accustomed to taking orders from small states and rejected the Bulgarian demand.

The Bulgarian position was difficult. The army had been mobilised since the end of the last summer but had done little fighting since November. The men were becoming restless, the more so as the sowing season was approaching. At the same time it was clear that the Serbs and the

The Bulgarians regarded Salonica as the natural outlet for their trade. The Greeks insisted that it was part of the historic Greek world. The largest ethnic group in the city was neither Bulgarian nor Greek but Jewish. The latter were descendants of Jews expelled from Spain in the 1490s and still spoke Ladino, a language derived from Spanish. In 1912 the Bulgarian army put as many Jewish soldiers as possible in the units which were sent to take the city. The city's Jewish community was destroyed in the Second World War.

Greeks had come to an agreement which led some Bulgarians to argue for a pre-emptive strike; the Bulgarian army had won stunning victories in the campaign against the Ottoman army and there was confidence that it would be more than a match for the combined Greek and Serbian forces, besides which a forward move by Bulgaria would force the Greeks and Serbs to come to the negotiating table in a submissive frame of mind. On 16 June 1913 the Bulgarians attacked their former allies. The Second Balkan War had begun.

This short but vicious conflict caused more casualties than the war against the Ottomans and it resulted in the total defeat of Bulgaria. The main reason for this was that when the Bulgarian army moved forward so too did the forces of Romania and the Ottoman Empire. Sofia was defenceless against the Romanian advance and there was no alternative to capitulation. In the Treaty of Bucharest in July Bulgaria lost almost all its gains in the west, retaining only the mountainous area of Pirin Macedonia; it was also forced to surrender the entire southern Dobrudja to Romania. In the Treaty of Constantinople with the Ottoman Empire in September Bulgaria lost much of the territory it had conquered in Thrace, retaining only a thin coastal strip which included the port of Dedeagach (Alexandroupolis).

> 'The Bulgars are brutes, but they certainly got less than they deserved out of the Balkan war.'
> DUFF COOPER[3]

When General Savov had ordered the attack on 16 June he had been overruled by the prime minister, Stoyan Danev, only to have that order countermanded by the king who was commander-in-chief of the armed forces. Danev was then sacked. This tragedy of errors was to some degree the result of personality clashes but it could not have happened without the personal regime. Whatever its causes the disaster of 1913 meant that Macedonia had once again been lost and that in an attempt to regain it Bulgaria would twice align with the losing side in world wars of the 20th century.

Stamboliĭski's opposition to what had initially been a popular war had been a setback for the BANU which was further damaged by strict government censorship of the press, and even if some activists worried the military commanders by setting up *druzhbi* in army units, the Union emerged from the wars a weakened force. It soon recuperated. Stamboliĭski was even more opposed to war in 1913 than he had been in 1912 and the Second Balkan War made his anti-war message more credible. That message had become more strident. On the first anniversary of the outbreak of the Second Balkan War Stamboliĭski told a student demonstration organised by the BANU in front of the sŭbranie building that, *Of those responsible for the catastrophe, Ferdinand is the most guilty; he should be strung up head downwards in front of the statue of the Tsar Liberator*.[4] Popular anger at the Second Balkan War had already been registered in the elections of November 1913, the first to be held under nation-wide PR; they returned 48 BANU deputies in an assembly of 204. The opposition deputies outnumbered those of the government whose leader, the pro-German Vasil Radoslavov, held another election in March 1914. Despite the massive deployment of government influence Radoslavov's party had exactly the same number of deputies as the opposition. The latter included 50 agrarians.

In the summer of 1914 attention once again became focused on international affairs. At the outbreak of the First World War Radoslavov's government declared 'strict and loyal neutrality'. Radoslavov and Ferdinand were thought to lean towards the Central Powers but the country was war weary and had no stomach for yet another fight. For a year Bulgaria was content to be courted by both sides. It was a valuable asset. Its army was still large and powerful, it controlled the supply lines from Germany and Austria-Hungary to their Ottoman ally, and if

'This warlike and powerful Bulgaria, with its scheming King and its valiant peasant armies, brooding over what seemed to them intolerable wrongs was the dominant factor in the Balkans in 1914 and 1915.'
WINSTON CHURCHILL[5]

Bulgaria chose to commit itself to one side or the other Greece and Romania would in all probability follow suit.

In August 1914 Stamboliĭski had approved of the declaration of neutrality, stating that: *This policy of the folded hands, of peace, is approved by the entire Bulgarian nation, because it guarantees us enhanced tranquillity for the present and the future, and because it will bring us greater benefits in that uncertain future. The Bulgarian nation is exhausted; it needs a rest...* . But he went on to warn, *We most emphatically call upon the government not to give way to any kind of foreign influence, not to have recourse to any measures for mobilisation, and not to infringe the neutrality it has declared.*[6] Stamboliĭski did not object to the acquisition of Bulgarian-populated lands in Macedonia and Romania: *if it is achievable,* he told the sŭbranie, *ask for it; if it is not then do not reject that which is offered as the price of neutrality.*[7] But not even the goal of full national unity justified the use of anything but peaceful means; his party was *not opposed to the unification of Bulgaria ... but to us the blood of Bulgaria's sons is more dear and more precious than any form of unification or expansion.*[8]

In the summer of 1915 Ferdinand and Radoslavov, fulfilling Stamboliĭski's worst fears, decided to commit Bulgaria to the German side. For this there were two main reasons. The first was that the Germans seemed to be the more likely victors; the Allies had made no progress on the Western Front, they were facing defeat in Gallipoli and in the east the Russians were in headlong retreat. The second was that the Germans could offer more than the Allies. The Bulgarians wanted Macedonia but this the Allies had promised to Serbia. The Germans could offer the whole of Macedonia and more once Serbia had been defeated. Unfortunately for the Allies it was far easier for the Central Powers to promise Bulgaria what belonged to their enemy than it was for the Allies to promise what belonged to their friend. Secret treaties were concluded between Bulgaria and the Central Powers in August and September and at the end of the latter month Bulgaria entered the war on the German side. Its reward was to be all of Serbian Macedonia together with some Serbian territory on the left bank of the River Morava.

Shortly before the declaration of war the main opposition parties were summoned to audiences with the prime minister and the king. From the remarks of the former it was assumed that the decision to commit Bulgaria to the German side had already been taken. Stamboliĭski told the king, *Everything which I and my fellow agrarian deputies have learned absolutely convinces me that what your government is contemplating is frightful, terrible and catastrophic – and not just because of its content but also because there are not the necessary conditions to carry it through to a satisfactory outcome.* Stamboliĭski then enumerated the reasons why the policy would not work and, looking straight into his eyes, warned Ferdinand, *but most important of all, the faith of the nation in You, Your Majesty, is completely shaken and destroyed. In its eyes, in the eyes of the nation, after the disaster of 16 June 1913, you have lost your reputation as shrewd diplomat.* He added later, *Remember, however, if tomorrow You carry out this criminal act we in the Agrarian Union will not only not restrain the popular anger against You, we will become the vehicle for its expression and we will serve upon You its heavy but just sentence.* When the king remarked that Stamboliĭski was very direct in what he said Stamboliĭski replied, *I am telling you what you have to be told.*[9] Finally Stamboliĭski warned Ferdinand that if he followed his chosen course, *you should think first of your head*. The king responded, 'Don't worry about my head. I am old. Think of your own which is still young.' [10]

Stamboliĭski spent the rest of that day and the following night writing a pamphlet describing his audience with the king and calling upon the people and especially the army to refuse to participate in the war. This was tantamount to treason but despite the pleas of senior colleagues Stamboliĭski refused to retract or to withdraw the pamphlet. Most copies were seized by the military police and Stamboliĭski was deprived of his seat in parliament and sentenced to death for treason, though Ferdinand commuted the sentence to life imprisonment. Stamboliĭski was sent to a not too uncomfortable cell in Sofia central prison where he could continue writing and maintain his contacts with party leaders. He also kept fit by constant physical exercise. The absence of their leader, however, crippled the BANU deputies in the sŭbranie and in December they joined with the government and other opposition parties to vote for war credits. Ferdinand and Radoslavov were free to pursue their war.

The Bulgarian army had already joined the victorious Central Powers onslaught on Serbia. The Bulgarian high command were keen to press on into Greek Macedonia with Salonica as their chief objective, but this the Germans forbad, arguing that Allied troops driven out of Macedonia would be redeployed on the Western Front. An advance into Greek Macedonia was sanctioned in the spring of 1916 but it made little progress. At the end of August 1916 Romania succumbed to pressure from the Allies and joined the war on their side. It met with little military success and in September was conquered from the north by German and Austro-Hungarian troops and from the south by Ottoman and Bulgarian forces.

There were not to be major changes in the disposition of the armies in the Balkans until September 1918. But, for Stamboliĭski, the tide had turned almost a year earlier with Russia's exit from the war. He greeted the New Year in 1918 with optimism: *An understanding between Bulgaria and Russia, between the two Slav nations so close in language and blood, between the liberator and the liberated, who have by the malign will of destiny taken up the sword against each other, is already an accomplished fact... . The new year thus begins its first days well enough. For the first time in a number of years the sound of the Christmas bell chimes with the millions of human voices raised in the call for Peace upon Earth.*[11]

But the nine long months before Bulgaria was to be at peace brought the greatest social suffering known in the country since liberation.

5
Bulgaria's Exit from the War

The breakdown of the military stalemate in the Balkans began with an Allied attack launched on 15 September 1918. Within a week the Bulgarian army was in rapid retreat towards Bulgaria itself. On 25 September British and French troops entered the country. A crown council decided to seek an armistice and a delegation was despatched to the front line. The armistice was signed in Salonica on 29 September. Hostilities were to cease at noon the following day; all Bulgarian units west of Skopje were to become prisoners of war; the remainder of the Bulgarian forces were to return to Bulgaria and demobilise immediately with the exception of three divisions which were to guard the railways and the Turkish border; the Allies were to have the rights to use all transport facilities in Bulgaria and to occupy any strategic point; all German and Austrian subjects were to leave Bulgaria in four weeks; and all Allied prisoners were to be handed over immediately. It was also made clear that though the Coburg dynasty might remain, Ferdinand had to abdicate. Bulgaria had been the last state to join the Central Powers and was the first to leave them; Ludendorff, the Quartermaster General of the German army and an influential advisor to the Chief of the General Staff, Paul von Hindenburg, admitted in his memoirs that it was the Bulgarian collapse which convinced him that the Central Powers could not win the war and that an armistice had to be sought.[1]

One cause of the Bulgarian collapse was the appointment of the energetic General Franchet d'Esperey as the commander of the Allied army at Salonica. He was helped by the addition to his forces of fresh and vigorous Greek forces whose advance west of the River Vardar had alerted the Allied high command to the possibility of success in an area which had until then been discounted on the assumption that the troops in Salonica were too weakened by malaria to be of any use.

But there were long term and more fundamental reasons for the Bulgarian collapse. The Russian Revolution of February 1917 had removed tsarist autocracy and therefore made it even less palatable for the russophile Bulgarians to have to fight against the Russians; indeed, many of them refused to do so and there was a series of mutinies in regiments facing the Russian army. Stamboliĭski immediately saw also that the elimination of the Russian autocracy would mean the United States would enter the war on the Allied side. When it did so defeat for the Central Powers would be inevitable and therefore Bulgaria should seek a separate peace immediately. Stamboliĭski conveyed this message to the many soldiers he came into contact with, either because they were detained in Sofia prison or because they visited him there. So effective was his propaganda that in September 1917 the government decided to remove him from the relaxed regime of Sofia central prison and lock him up in the fortress of Vidin in the far north-west of Bulgaria.

It made little difference. His message became ever more relevant and influential. In January 1916 Radoslavov had defined Bulgaria's war aims as the desire to unite all Bulgarians in one state and this seemed to have been achieved. Why, then, asked many, and not least the anti-war agrarians and their leader, not seek a separate peace? When Bulgarian troops were required by the Germans to cross the Danube into indisputably Romanian territory some members of the Bulgarian opposition denounced the move on the grounds that this was not fighting for national unity but open aggression. The announcement of President Wilson's Fourteen Points in January 1918 intensified this feeling. The 11th of those Points called for borders based on historically determined lines of nationality; if the US President wanted a peace based on ethnic principles, why not seek it immediately, the more because Bulgaria was not at war with the USA which many Bulgarians believed would look favourably on their country.

In 1918, to many Bulgarians, it seemed they had more to fear from their supposed friends than their putative enemies. Early in the year the Germans ended their financial subsidies to Bulgaria and in March reduced supplies of arms and other military equipment. Furthermore, as Stamboliĭski had foreseen, the arrival of American troops gravely weakened the Germans on the Western Front and a number of units were therefore withdrawn from the Balkans and sent to France. But it was less in military than in political terms that Bulgaria came to suspect her co-belligerents.

The Allies seemed to be offering a peace based on Bulgaria's war aims, but the country's own partners seemed to be doing the opposite. In 1918 the Austrians requested the cession of the Vranya triangle in Serbia, and then the Ottoman government demanded the return of territory it had ceded to

Bulgaria in 1915. Constantinople's stance was supported by Germany; if the Germans were prepared to back the Turks in this, some Bulgarians asked, would they not be equally willing to sacrifice Bulgarian interests in Thrace and Macedonia should the pro-German Constantine retrieve his throne in Athens? And worst of all was the position in the north.

Bulgaria had always regarded the Dobrudja as part of *Bulgaria irredenta* and to many it seemed the least contentious of Bulgaria's territorial aspirations. But when the area was conquered by the Central Powers it was not allocated to Bulgaria but divided, the northern half being placed under the joint administration of the Central Powers with Bulgaria taking over the southern section. Even Radoslavov admitted that Bulgaria had been treated more like a defeated foe than an ally.

The failure to secure all of the Dobrudja impacted on the prime cause of Bulgaria's collapse in 1918. The Dobrudja was a rich grain-growing area and it had been hoped that its acquisition would help alleviate the intensifying problems of food supply. These had been with the Bulgarian government since it joined the war. The army had to be provided with weapons, ammunition, food and clothing but at the same time the civilian population, in Bulgaria and the occupied territories, also had to be fed and clothed. The difficulties were considerable. Mobilisation had taken most able-bodied men from the fields where work was increasingly carried out by women, the young, the old and the infirm. Crop yields inevitably declined. One result of this was the substitution of other products for grain in the making of bread; so awful had this become by the summer of 1918 that it was causing illness and even death amongst soldier and civilian alike.

A further problem was that large numbers of draft animals

PRESIDENT WILSON'S FOURTEEN POINTS, 8 JANUARY 1918

The program of the world's peace, therefore, is our program; and that program, the only possible program, as we see it, is this:

I. Open covenants of peace, openly arrived at, after which there shall be no private international understandings of any kind but diplomacy shall proceed always frankly and in the public view.

II. Absolute freedom of navigation upon the seas, outside territorial waters, alike in peace and in war, except as the seas may be closed in whole or in part by international action for the enforcement of international covenants.

III. The removal, so far as possible, of all economic barriers and the establishment of an equality of trade conditions among all the nations consenting to the peace and associating themselves for its maintenance.

IV. Adequate guarantees given and taken that national armaments will be reduced to the lowest point consistent with domestic safety.

V. A free, open-minded, and absolutely impartial adjustment of all colonial claims, based upon a strict observance of the principle that in determining all such questions of sovereignty the interests of the populations concerned must have equal weight with the equitable claims of the government whose title is to be determined.

VI. The evacuation of all Russian territory and such a settlement of all questions affecting Russia as will secure the best and freest cooperation of the other nations of the world in obtaining for her an unhampered and unembarrassed opportunity for the independent determination of her own political development and national policy and assure her of a sincere welcome into the society of free nations under institutions of her own choosing; and, more than a welcome, assistance also of every kind that she may need and may herself desire. The treatment accorded Russia by her sister nations in the months to come will be the acid test of their good will, of their comprehension of her needs as distinguished from their own interests, and of their intelligent and unselfish sympathy.

VII. Belgium, the whole world will agree, must be evacuated and restored, without any attempt to limit the sovereignty which she enjoys in common with all other free nations. No other single act will serve as this will serve to restore confidence among the nations in the laws which they have themselves set and determined for the government of their relations with one another. Without this healing act the whole structure and validity of international law is forever impaired.

VIII. All French territory should be freed and the invaded portions restored, and the wrong done to France by Prussia in 1871 in the matter of Alsace-Lorraine, which has unsettled the peace of the world for nearly fifty years, should be righted, in order that peace may once more be made secure in the interest of all.

IX. A readjustment of the frontiers of Italy should be effected along clearly recognizable lines of nationality.

X. The peoples of Austria-Hungary, whose place among the nations we wish to see safeguarded and assured, should be accorded the freest opportunity to autonomous development.

XI. Rumania, Serbia, and Montenegro should be evacuated; occupied territories restored; Serbia accorded free and secure access to the sea; and the relations of the several Balkan states to one another determined by friendly counsel along historically established lines of allegiance and nationality; and international guarantees of the political and economic independence and territorial integrity of the several Balkan states should be entered into.

XII. The Turkish portion of the present Ottoman Empire should be assured a secure sovereignty, but the other nationalities which are now under Turkish rule should be assured an undoubted security of life and an absolutely unmolested opportunity of autonomous development, and the Dardanelles should be permanently opened as a free passage to the ships and commerce of all nations under international guarantees.

XIII. An independent Polish state should be erected which should include the territories inhabited by indisputably Polish populations, which should be assured a free and secure access to the sea, and whose political and economic independence and territorial integrity should be guaranteed by international covenant.

XIV. A general association of nations must be formed under specific covenants for the purpose of affording mutual guarantees of political independence and territorial integrity to great and small states alike.

had also been mobilised, not least because the Bulgarian army in the south was strung out on a long, mainly mountainous front which had few decent roads and virtually no railways; pack animals had to be used extensively and they could be found only by requisitioning them from the peasants. A further, and very unpopular factor was that the Germans and the Austrians had been granted the right to take fixed quantities of Bulgarian food; to help them do this the Germans had taken control of Bulgaria's railways and telephone system and German currency had become legal tender in the country. The result was that the Germans and Austrians took far more than the permitted quantities. And very often they were helped in doing so by corrupt Bulgarian politicians; one reported incident of this was the loading of 30,000 sheep onto a ship in Burgas harbour during a faked air-raid. Requisitioning by the Bulgarian authorities had been far from popular, but the taking of food and other commodities by the Germans was resented far more.

The Bulgarian Workers' Social Democratic Party was founded by a group of committed intellectuals in 1891. It did secure the election of a few deputies but the lack of a developed working class limited the party's potential. In 1903 it split between the 'Broads' and the 'Narrows', the former eventually becoming the Social Democratic Party (SDP) and the latter the Bulgarian Communist Party (BCP). The main dividing issue was the extent to which the party should work in parliament and with other political groups. The split also divided the nascent trade union movement.

Food prices inevitably rose. An index of the cost of a number of necessities measured at 100 in 1914 had reached 200 by 1916, 500 at the beginning of 1918, and 870 in July of that year. If price increases were inevitable so was the reaction to them. In December 1917 in Sofia 10,000 or more protesters cheered the Narrow Socialist leader Dimitŭr Blagoev when he demanded peace and revolution. More effective and more widespread protest came in the 'Women's Revolution' of May 1918 when half-starved women took to the streets in a number of towns in protest at the lack of food.

Of all the factors which sapped the morale of the army in 1918 it was the declining situation on the home front which did most to dishearten the peasant soldiers. They were tough characters who could bear enormous privation and who could live, albeit regretfully, with the fact that the Germans and Austrians who fought with them were better paid, better fed, better armed, better clothed, better shod and even better protected because the cement used to build their fortifications was superior to the Bulgarians'. But what they could not tolerate was what they saw when they went home in the summer of 1918 to help take in the harvest: that their women and children were virtually starving. Almost literally the Bulgarian soldier no longer had the stomach for the fight.

In June 1918 Radoslavov had resigned, the failure to secure control of all the Dobrudja being the main cause. His successor was Aleksandŭr Malinov. The leader of the Democratic Party knew the mood of the country and that the most powerful political force was that of the peasantry. He wanted a coalition government which would include the agrarians and in the hope that their leader might persuade the BANU to join with him he had Stamboliĭski brought back from Vidin to the central prison in Sofia. But Stamboliĭski would take the agrarians into government only on certain conditions, the most important of which was that Bulgaria should immediately leave the war. The king was not prepared to do this. Malinov therefore had to govern without Stamboliĭski. The weakness of his administration may be gauged from the fact that when, in July, he secured control of the northern Dobrudja this major concession did nothing to placate the rising anger in the military and at home. By the middle of the summer desertion rates in the army were increasing and the disaffected soldiers were establishing links with the radical parties, above all the agrarians. Malinov approached the Allies but they were not receptive.[2] When the Macedonian front disintegrated in the middle of September Malinov could no longer afford to keep Stamboliĭski confined to prison and he was released and asked to do what he could to calm the army. He agreed but only on condition that Bulgaria accepted whatever terms the Allies chose to dictate for the armistice. Once again Malinov was powerless to resist; not only had the front collapsed and Allied forces entered Bulgaria but his own troops appeared to be about to stage a revolution.

Days of confusion followed. The focus of the disorders was Radomir where troops pouring home from the broken front concentrated. Radomir, some 25 miles south-west of Sofia, was also within striking range of General Staff Headquarters at Kyustendil. The defeated troops were in an ugly mood and they were backed by a leading agrarian, Raĭko Daskalov, named by Stamboliĭski as head of a provisional government. Some days of indecision and confusion followed. Daskalov judged the army of the revolution strong enough to take Sofia and proposed to Stamboliĭski that they put themselves at the head of the troops and march on the capital. Stamboliĭski was non-committal but he did little or nothing to deter Daskalov who duly set off in the direction of Sofia. He was not to reach it. By the evening he was at the edge of the city but then made a number of errors, failing to launch an attack until the following morning and failing, too, to cut off Sofia's lines of communication to the north. This enabled the government to concentrate loyal forces, mainly Macedonian units and some hastily brought in German troops, around the city and these proved strong enough to blunt the rebel attack. Stamboliĭski now insisted that he had no connection with the rebellion and that Daskalov had only put himself at the head of it because the mutinous soldiery had left him no alternative. This carried little conviction and Stamboliĭski's next move was to try and bring about a rising within Sofia in aid of the rebel army and with the further aim of bringing about a full-scale national revolt. His effort failed. He sought the cooperation of the Narrow Socialists, soon to reconstitute themselves as the Bulgarian Communist Party (BCP), but they were convinced full-scale revolution on the bolshevik model was around the corner and they had no need of cooperation with petit bourgeois peasants. It was not the last time hubris visited Bulgaria's would-be bolsheviks. Even if the Narrows had agreed to join Stamboliĭski, however, their prospects of success were dubious. The main demand of the discontented soldiers was peace and this by now had been achieved with the signing of the armistice at Salonica. And another major grievance was removed when it became known that the victorious Allies were insisting that Ferdinand leave the country. This he did, abdicating in favour of his son who became Boris III.

With the revolutionary emergency over it was time for political and social reconstruction. The country was subject to occupation by Allied forces but it was the local political authorities which had responsibility for administering it. There were serious problems. Food supplies were still limited and demobilisation produced pressures, particularly in the towns. Even more serious were the difficulties caused by the surge of refugees who came flooding in from Thrace, the Dobrudja and above all from Macedonia, following the armistice's insistence that Bulgaria withdraw from all the areas it had occupied during the war.

On the political front change was inevitable, but it was much less radical than had seemed likely in September. Malinov reconstructed his cabinet in October. It now included, in addition to the old parliamentary parties, agrarians and representatives of one socialist faction. However, Stamboliĭski, though undoubtedly the most influential politician in the country, was not included. Malinov left office in November in protest at the Allied insistence that Bulgaria withdraw from the southern Dobrudja, and was succeeded as prime minister by Teodor Teodorov who, in January 1919, at last brought Stamboliĭski into the government; he was made minister of public works.

Elections were not held until August 1919 and in them the old parties still retained two-fifths of the votes. The remaining 60 per cent were divided more or less equally between the agrarians and the two socialist groups. A coalition was not finalised until October and this time Stamboliĭski was at its head. It had taken so long to form the coalition because Stamboliĭski had again tried to bring about an alliance with the other leftist factions, but once more the communists had refused to join with the petit bourgeois class enemy. Stamboliĭski therefore had to rely on members of two of the old parliamentary parties, the Progressive Liberals and the Nationalists. It was becoming clear in Bulgaria that the war had gravely weakened but had not destroyed the old political system, but who was going to step into the widening gap caused by their weakening was by no means obvious. The two contestants were the major forces on the left, the BANU and the BCP, and the contest between them was to dominate internal affairs for the next six months.

Inevitably, in the immediate future, the main preoccupation was not domestic conflict but the impending peace treaty.

The Bulgarians were not entirely depressed. They took great solace from the Wilsonian doctrines of national self-determination, and there were other encouraging signs, not the least being the fact that the 1917 enquiry on which Wilson had relied heavily in formulating his views had stated that the settlement after the Second Balkan War was unjust, that its continuation would endanger peace, that the southern Dobrudja should be returned to Bulgaria, the Bulgarian-Turkish border should follow the Enos-Midia line, that Bulgaria should retain direct access to the Aegean via western Thrace, and that the Macedonian question should be settled by an independent enquiry. In May 1919 Bulgaria requested a peace on such a basis.[3]

Stamboliĭski was amongst those who believed a new world would be built on Wilsonian principles and that Bulgaria would not be subjected to condign punishment because it had now cast off the royalist clique and its pro-German lackeys who had taken an unwilling country to war. The new Bulgaria, soon to be built on agrarian foundations, would be a welcome member of the new community and would take part in it enthusiastically. As Stamboliĭski had written in *The Principles of the BANU, The Agrarian Union is for lasting, peaceful, neighbourly relations between Bulgaria and the surrounding states.*[4] And it would press for a new Balkan federation to preserve the peace.

It was in this relatively up-beat frame of mind that the Bulgarian delegation set off for Paris in July 1919. Stamboliĭski is said to have spent much of the time looking out of the train window and comparing the varying forms of cultivation.[5]

The delegation was headed by the prime minister Todorov, a conservative russophile who distrusted all radicals, Stamboliĭski included. Also in the delegation were

Yanko Sakŭzov, a socialist, Mihail Ganev, a member of the Radical Party, and Stamboliĭski. Their professional advisor was Dimitŭr Stanciov, a sophisticated career diplomat whose monocle was said to have bemused Stamboliĭski.[6] Their chief of propaganda was a figure cut from a very different cloth. Kosta Todorov had fought in the war, but with the French Foreign Legion rather than the Bulgarian army, and in 1916 he had returned to Bulgaria with a peace proposal from the French commander. For this he was thrown into prison where he became a close associate of Stamboliĭski. The delegation, quite deliberately in view of the importance being attached to the protection of minorities, included representatives from all five major religions in Bulgaria: Orthodoxy, Catholicism, Protestantism, Judaism and Islam.

Whatever confidence the delegation had in the peace process was soon to be roughly dispelled.

Bulgaria's fate is about to be communicated to its delegation, Neuilly-sur-Seine, 1919.

II
The Paris Peace Conference

6
The Treaty of Neuilly

When the Bulgarian delegation crossed the border into France its two female members were presented with bouquets of flowers in the Bulgarian national colours.[1] But when they arrived in Paris on 26 July the reception was very different; in the words of the first British historian of the peace conference, the Bulgarians 'seem to have been surprised that no one offered to shake hands with them.'[2] The second encounter was the more accurate omen. The delegation was taken to the Château de Madrid in Neuilly and forbidden to visit Paris. They were to be watched by detectives who would accompany them should they wish to walk in the adjacent woods or shop in the nearby town. All their correspondence was to be censored and they were not to receive visitors, even family members. The delegation was to be charged for the hire of the furniture and each individual member would have to pay for his or her meals.[3] It was possible, however, to escape occasionally and Stamboliĭski found some relief from boredom in clandestine meetings with Kosta Todorov either rowing on lakes in the Bois de Boulogne or, improbably for the irreligious Stamboliĭski, at services in a Russian Orthodox Church.

The delegation remained in this state of semi-incarceration for two months. They then had to return to Bulgaria following the elections in August after which Stamboliĭski was preoccupied with engineering the coalition which was to take office in October. One of the first acts of the new, agrarian-dominated government was to arrest members of the Rado-slavov cabinet. This was a popular measure at home and was also intended to show the Allies that Bulgaria had rejected its recent past and therefore did not deserve harsh punishment. This did not work.

The Bulgarians were ordered to reappear in Paris on 19 October to hear the terms of the treaty. They were worse than anything the Bulgarians had feared. The Bulgarians asked for ten days in which to prepare their response and this they were granted. Their appeal was heard on 24 October. Its chief point was that Bulgaria had changed and was now a peaceful and democratic country, but this had little effect. Some amendments were made to the financial clauses and the Allies accepted the Bulgarian argument that some of the provisions regarding minorities were otiose because they were already included in the Bulgarian constitution. On the territorial and military stipulations, however, the Allies remained inflexible. The delegation then returned to Sofia where Todorov announced that he could not put his name to such a treaty and resigned as head of the Bulgarian delegation. The young king, on the other hand, saw, as did many others, that Bulgaria was in no position to resist and that there was no alternative to acceptance. More importantly, this was also Stamboliĭski's view. He took the courageous decision that he would return to Paris and that he alone would sign the treaty to end the war he had been imprisoned for opposing.

When he returned to Paris Stamboliĭski made a final effort

to ameliorate the terms of the treaty. He wrote to Clemenceau and to the heads of the Greek, Romanian and Serbian delegations pointing out once more his own constant opposition to the war and insisting that his government would follow entirely peaceful policies. He also called for a new approach to inter-Balkan relations which should now be based on conciliation and cooperation. In his letter to the head of the Romanian delegation he stated: *The fearful suffering which the peoples of the Balkans have endured in recent years, I believe, lays especial obligations upon the statesmen of the region to work towards mutual accommodation and full agreement between their states. On them, and especially on the statesmen of the victorious nations, depends, on the eve of the signing of peace with Bulgaria, whether the peoples of our tormented peninsula will iron out for ever the lamentable disagreements which until now have prevented them from enjoying the blessing of a political organisation coming together at a higher level, or to bridge the gaps which yawn between them and which for long years have held them in a state of enmity one to another. I have always been a passionate advocate of the idea of mutual agreements between the Balkan states. I have suffered for that idea, but I have never doubted its feasibility or its beneficial effect. And now when my country, made impotent by wars, has entrusted me with its fate, I feel more than ever duty bound to raise my voice in defence of this idea…. .*[4]

Pleading that the Bulgarian people ought not to suffer for the sins of their former leaders, he asked each government to consider the principle of national self-determination before pressing its demands. Generosity now, he argued, could form the basis of a lasting Balkan peace.[5] The letters had no effect. On 27 November in the Marie in Neuilly Stamboliĭski signed the treaty. It was to be ratified by the Bulgarian parliament on 12 January 1920.

Stamboliĭski had been the only Bulgarian to sign the dreaded document but he made it clear that he did not take on the sole responsibility for doing so; he was not going to give his political enemies ammunition to attack him as a traitor; *I signed*, he wrote, *for the entire Bulgarian nation and the treaty is binding upon it. I will not allow anyone to contest the fact that this treaty, however harsh and unjust it might be towards Bulgaria, had to be signed, because the only alternative was continuation of the war, and no one is thinking of that.*[6]

ooooo

Part I of the Treaty of Neuilly was the standard set of clauses dealing with the League of Nations; Part II defined Bulgaria's new borders; Part III comprised the 'Political Clauses' regulating Bulgaria's relations with its neighbours, including, in section iv, the question of minority protection; Part IV dealt with military and naval matters; Part V concerned prisoners of war and war graves; the three articles (118–120) of Part VI set out the procedures for punishing those guilty of war crimes; Part VII covered repatriations; the financial clauses were collected in Part VIII; the lengthy and complex Part IX contained the economic clauses; aerial navigation was the subject of Part X; and Ports, Waterways and Railways were that of Part Xl; Part XII reproduced the clauses concerning Labour which were in Part XIII of the treaty of Versailles; Neuilly's final section, Part XIII, consisted of a series of miscellaneous clauses dealing with matters as diverse as regulating guarantees given to Switzerland in 1815 and the use of income from property belonging to Christian religious institutions. Bulgarian discontent concentrated on Parts II (territorial), IV (military) and VII (reparations).

The treaty did grant a small area to the north-west of Adrianople to Bulgaria. This was because the population of the enclave was predominantly Bulgarian, but this consideration did not mean that the southern Dobrudja was returned to Bulgaria. Handed to Romania in the settlement of 1913 the area was widely acknowledged to be predominantly Bulgarian by ethnicity; even the fiercely anti-Bulgarian Winston Churchill did not oppose its retention by Bulgaria at the end of the Second World War. In the west Bulgaria was to relinquish all its war-time gains in the Morava valley and in Macedonia. Indeed, Macedonia was not discussed at Neuilly and was not included in the treaty. There was worse to come. Not only did Bulgaria fail to retain any part of Macedonia, it was to lose three salients on its western border despite the fact that the majority of their populations were Bulgarians. Worst of all, in territorial terms, was that western Thrace should be put under Allied administration until a decision was taken at a later date as to its ultimate destiny. It was also stipulated (Article 48) that, 'The Principal Allied and Associated Powers undertake to ensure the economic outlets of Bulgaria to the Aegean Sea. The conditions of this guarantee will be fixed at a later date.' This gave Stamboliĭski and future Bulgarian leaders a lever with which to open discussions on the treaty.

The Bulgaria of 1915 had been 47,750 square miles in extent with a population of 5.5 million; in 1921 the figures were 45,000 square miles and a population of 5.2 million. The lost western territories contained 90,000 Bulgarians and in Macedonia there were probably a million who considered themselves Bulgarian.

The military clauses limited the 'the total number of rifles in use in Bulgaria' to 33,000. Of these 20,000 were to be held by soldiers in the army, 10,000 were to be in the hands of 'gendarmes, customs officials, forest guards, local or municipal police or other like officials', and a further 3,000 were to be held by a special corps of frontier guards. The treaty with Bulgaria was the only one which regulated the number of rifles, and this was to ensure that arms were not carried by unofficial organisations; even the Boy Scouts were denied the right to have arms (Article 74); Neuilly was 'the only Treaty in which they receive the honour of mention'.[7] Bulgaria was not required to destroy war materiel but to give it to the Allies. The treaty imposed an outright ban on conscription and Bulgaria's army was to be a volunteer force with officers serving 20 consecutive years and NCOs and men 12 consecutive years; the use of the word consecutive was a rejection of a Bulgarian request that soldiers be allowed to serve half their time with the colours and half in the reserve; the proportion of officers, including those on the staff and in special services, was not to exceed 5 per cent of the total number of men with the colours, and no more than one in five officers was to be allowed to resign their commissions in any one year. There were to be no military exercises, theoretical or practical, and there was to be no air force, and no general staff. No military unit larger than a division was to be allowed and there was to be a prohibition on the 'formation of any other group of forces, as well as any other organisation concerned with military command or war preparation' (Article 68). Weapons were to be restricted and tables were compiled illustrating the permitted maxima. The treaty left Bulgaria four torpedo boats, three of which were damaged, which were to be used for police purposes and whose armament was to be limited to one light gun, and six motor boats, four of which were damaged. One gunboat was to be sold for the benefit of the Allies and one submarine was to be handed over to Britain.

The Allies recognised that Bulgaria, after almost ten years of war, was not in a position to make complete reparation for the damage they believed it had caused. Nevertheless, the total sum demanded, 225 million gold francs or £90,000,000, was hefty, and it was to be paid in half-yearly instalments over the next 38 years. In addition to money payments Bulgaria was to deliver to Serbia 50,000 tons of coal per year for the next five years. Within six months of the treaty coming into force Bulgaria was to hand over to Greece, Romania and the Kingdom of the Serbs, Croats and Slovenes (Yugoslavia) railway equipment and stipulated numbers of bulls, milch cows, horses, mares, mules, draught oxen and sheep. The payment of reparations was to be organised and supervised by a reparations commission.

The Bulgarians had hoped that the Bulgarian people would not be punished for policies with which they had not agreed, and that the peace would be drawn up on Wilsonian principles. The Allies, however, rejected the notion that the Bulgarian nation as a whole had been opposed to the war, and the treaty was determined less by Wilsonian principles than by strategic and military considerations. The Bulgarians had been at fault. They were to be punished and they were to be prevented from carrying out any further aggression against their neighbours.

For those drawing up the treaty Bulgaria's main crime had been to prolong the war. Its first sins were of omission rather than commission. Bulgaria controlled the three rail lines from the Ottoman Empire to Europe; by remaining neutral, or at least by not supervising those lines more vigilantly, it allowed supplies to flow unimpeded between Germany and Turkey. Nor had Bulgaria prevented the use of the Danube to ferry arms and other materials between Germany and the Ottoman Empire. The sin of commission came in September 1915 with the attack on Serbia. Here communications were again important. When the Ottoman Empire joined the Central Powers the sea route between the Western Allies and Russia had been closed but at least there remained the difficult land routes via Greece, Serbia, Bulgaria and Romania. Now these too were closed; supplies to Russia could be taken only by long sea journeys, as a result of which Russia was seriously, perhaps mortally, weakened. The Bulgarian entry into the war had also, it was argued, perhaps casuistically, increased the difficulties the Allies were facing in Gallipoli and thereafter had kept three-quarters of a million Allied troops in Salonica when they could have been used to force a conclusion on the vital Western Front.

The treaty was to ensure that Bulgaria was rendered incapable of further aggression. The first means to this end were indirect, by increasing the size and strategic significance of the other states whilst decreasing those of Bulgaria. It was strategic considerations, therefore, which dictated the alienation of the salients on Bulgaria's western border. The areas lost were those from which Bulgaria could threaten rail and road links between Yugoslavia and Greece.

In the case of Thrace strategy again ruled the day. Bulgaria was to be allowed an economic outlet but it was not to have a foothold on the Aegean coast because from there it might be able to threaten Constantinople and the Straits. The conference believed that 'it was imperatively necessary to cover the supremely important position of Constantinople and the Straits against future ambitious movement from the north-west, and at the same time diminish the strategic importance of Bulgaria'.[8] There was a further consideration. If the Bulgarians were established on the Aegean coast they could threaten communications not only between the Greek mainland and the Greek islands, but also the supply lines to the projected new Greek territories in Asia Minor; therefore Bulgarian 'possession of the Aegean littoral would confer upon Bulgaria strategic advantages destructive of the larger purposes of the Conference'.[9] The Allies consoled themselves by noting that the Bulgarians did not form the ethnic majority in western Thrace where, in fact, all that could be said with certainty was that there was no clear ethnic majority and that Muslims outnumbered Christians. The Allies also argued that the new border along the watershed of the southern Rhodopes was more or less coterminous with the southern limits of Bulgarian ethnic domination.

Naturally the Bulgarians had deployed every conceivable argument against the treaty. They had played the ethnic card over the Dobrudja to no avail and it had proved equally ineffective with regarded to the lost salients in the west. The Bulgarians had tried to secure plebiscites for Macedonia, the western salients and Thrace; but they were denied a privilege granted to other defeated states. In Thrace the ethnic argument could not be used and the economic one was blunted by the offer, however ill-defined, of an economic outlet on the Aegean, though Bulgaria's reasonable insistence that no access could be secure which ran through foreign territory went unheeded.

If the territorial clauses were an indirect means to curtail Bulgaria's capacity to make war, the direct means were to be seen in the stipulations over reparations and the limitations to be placed on Bulgaria's armed forces. Reparations were also considered a direct means of punishment; indeed it was intended that reparations such as the handing-over of livestock were to be simple and clear so that the peasant could understand his nation was being chastised.

On the military question the Bulgarians' arguments were more detailed and practical, though equally ineffective. The Bulgarians requested a conscript army because, they argued, the nation's peasants would never consent to leave their villages and fields for so protracted a period as 12 or 20 years. That being so, a volunteer army would inevitably be raised primarily in the urban centres. These were highly radical, and usually socialist. In times of a bolshevik menace this was surely the least appropriate recruiting ground for a force which was to be 'exclusively employed for the maintenance of order within Bulgarian territory and for the control of the frontiers' (Article 66 (3)). There was even a question as to the commitment of the new officers who did not relish serving in a force with such minimal equipment and with nothing more glorious to contemplate than maintaining order at home. By the middle of 1920s it was reported that a number of officers were committing minor offences in the hope of being discharged for their misdemeanours.

The main reason why Stamboliĭski had signed the Treaty of Neuilly was that there was no practical alternative. But he also took solace from the belief that it could not last. When he had been sentenced to hard labour for life in November 1915, acting on an inner premonition, he had told his guards, *I shall be in prison for at the least three and at the most five years – that is as long as this war lasts.* Four years later when he was on his way to Paris he met at Tsaribrod on the Bulgarian-Yugoslav border a group of people expelled from their homes in territory occupied by and about to be given to

Yugoslavia. *They asked me, 'Is there any hope of reversing the loss of our homes?' I said, 'Yes, but a little later.' They asked, 'When, how long will we have to wait?' Again because of some inner premonition I answered calmly, 'Three years'. They were all satisfied with this answer. I signed the harsh treaty of peace in Paris because of my premonition which had hardened into conviction, that this treaty would not last more than three years.* Stamboliĭski was further convinced that, as after the Treaty of Berlin, the terms would be revised when it became apparent that they were unworkable, though he did not believe that revision would be brought about by force. Neuilly *will not be destroyed by the sword, of that I am absolutely certain. My prison chains were severed by raging national outrage, the chains put around Bulgaria by this treaty will be severed by an indignant world conscience. Of that too I am absolutely certain.*[10]

When Stamboliĭski had been released from prison in 1918 he had declared, *The greatest heroism is patience.*[11] Patience he had in abundance, and he used it in the protracted process of applying the treaty, not least over the question of the Aegean. His first move on the international scene was to tour a number of important European capitals once more to plead Bulgaria's case and to show that the new Bulgaria was a different country from the old.

But before he set out on his tour there were domestic problems to settle.

7

Stamboliĭski and the Restrictions of the Treaty of Neuilly

The impending peace treaty had overshadowed Bulgarian politics in the summer and autumn of 1919, but it had not stilled domestic strife. There was considerable social discontent, particularly in urban centres.

After the end of the fighting food had still been scarce and real famine had been avoided only by the large-scale importation of wheat, mainly from the USA. This had not prevented a rise in food prices which by the end of 1919 were 12 times higher than in 1914, and the requirement to deliver cattle and other livestock to Greece, Romania and Yugoslavia further diminished supplies and increased prices, notwithstanding the introduction of three meatless days per week in Sofia. The peasants could avoid the worst effects of food shortages by retreating further into self-sufficiency, but there was no such bolthole for the urban masses whose wages had risen only half as fast as prices. This affected everyone on fixed incomes, including pensioners and the many state employees, whilst the Allies' insistence in the armistice that Bulgaria's army be stood down had produced unemployment amongst the officer corps as well as a rapid and not easily absorbed demobilisation, in addition to which there were the mounting tensions created by the refugee influx. Discontent reached boiling point in July 1919 with a massive protest rally in Sofia.

The rising urban discontent deepened the gulf between the towns and the countryside and therefore threw into even sharper focus the cardinal fact of post-First World War politics in Bulgaria: that the two forces of the left would compete for the political vacuum created by the discrediting of the traditional parties. Partly in recognition of this fact, Stamboliĭski established a new force, the Orange Guard. Like many other organisations in Europe immediately after the First World War it was an armed adjunct to a political party, though in this case its arms, because of Allied pressure, were limited mostly to the traditional club. The sharpening rural/urban, agrarian/socialist divide produced another and very surprising result: cooperation between the two main socialist factions, the BCP and the SDP.

At the end of 1919 they combined to stage a general strike. The reaction of Stamboliĭski's government was fierce. The Orange Guard, as well as the police and the few soldiers still allowed to bear arms, were deployed against the strikers, and serving soldiers with experience in working the railways were mobilised to keep the trains moving. Even more effective were government threats to deprive strikers and their families of ration cards, or to evict them from their homes. The strike collapsed in January 1920, though the miners in Pernik did not go back to work for another six weeks. The government's tough measures had been too much, particularly in winter when fuel as well as food was short, and the link between the SDP and the BCP was fragile; the former had thrown in its lot with the strikers less from conviction than from a fear that not to join in would diminish its following amongst the workers.

When social tensions had subsided Stamboliĭski decided to turn his victory over the strikers to electoral advantage. He announced that a national poll would be held on 28 March 1920 but before it took place a new law was enacted making voting compulsory. The results were not quite what he had wanted. The agrarian vote was almost doubled but that of the communists went up by almost two-thirds; the former now had 110 seats in the assembly and the latter 51. It was not enough to give the BANU an absolute majority so to create the new order he wanted Stamboliĭski fell back on some traditional methods of electoral manipulation. The agrarians had already exercised some influence over the polls, now their leader played one of the oldest and dirtiest tricks in the Bulgarian parliamentary game: the election of 13 deputies, nine of them communists, was declared invalid, thus giving Stamboliĭski's party a majority of two. Stamboliĭski then formed what was the first non-coalition agrarian government in Europe. Nevertheless, the events of July 1919 to March 1920 raised a number of eyebrows.

∞∞∞∞

In the summer of 1920 Stamboliĭski set about implementing his party's domestic programme and by the autumn, with this process in train, and feeling confident that he was now secure in office, Stamboliĭski decided to set off on a 100-day tour of a number of European capitals. His objectives were to end Bulgaria's diplomatic isolation, to show Europe that a new Bulgaria had emerged from the war; and to bring that new Bulgaria into the European fold; in his own words he wished to prove that *Instead of the gun and the cannon we have slogans of peace, for friendly neighbourly relations*;[1] he also wanted to dispel the feeling that peasants such as he could not cut a proper figure in the international arena. In practical terms he wanted to scotch rumours current in parts of Europe that his regime was 'bolshevik', and to do what he could to secure implementation of Article 48 of Neuilly with regard to economic access to the Aegean.

Stamboliĭski was much excited by his tour and before leaving gave the British minister in Sofia 'the impression of a boy off for a holiday'.[2] He took with him a number of advisors, one of whom was Stanciov, and another of whom, an interpreter-secretary, was Stanciov's daughter, Nadezhda. She proved an able companion and in her translating was not averse to adding a little diplomatic finesse to Stamboliĭski's sometimes forthright remarks; it was observed more than once that her translations were longer than Stamboliĭski's original. Nadezhda and Stamboliĭski enjoyed a close relationship, a phrase which is not intended to convey that that relationship was anything other than platonic. Certainly Ms Stanciov admired her boss; she wrote privately to her family that, ' … nothing would astonish me about Stame [Aleksandûr], at one moment a child and the next a genius. (Yes, very simply and I am not joking.) He dazzles me sometimes with that immense intelligence!'[3]

The first, and most successful visit was to Great Britain, where the Bulgarian party arrived on 9 October. Two days later Stamboliĭski was received by the British foreign secretary, Lord Curzon. Here Stamboliĭski pressed the need for Bulgaria to have proper access to the Aegean and when Curzon responded that the British favoured the recent Greek suggestion that the Bulgarians should have access to the port of Dedeagach Stamboliĭski replied bluntly, *We believe in England, in the great powers, but we cannot have faith in the Greeks. A Bulgarian outlet to the sea cannot pass through Greek territory.*[4]

Winston Churchill, then secretary for war, also advised Stamboliĭski to work with the Greeks, not least, said Churchill, because their prime minister Venizelos was a great man.

> 'A stout-hearted patriot.'
> LORD CURZON ON STAMBOLIĬSKI[5]

Stamboliĭski agreed as to the Greek premier's ability but questioned his political longevity; wisely, it proved, because Venizelos was removed from office within a month. Stamboliĭski met with a number of other prominent figures but his most relaxed encounter was with the then prime minister, David Lloyd George. He and Stamboliĭski established a friendly, chaffing relationship. They were both figures who had risen from outside the political establishment and had taken up the cudgels against it, and in office both had had to face threats from the radical left. They found it possible to mix humour with business: when asked if Britain could take Macedonia under its wing as a mandate, Lloyd George replied he would do so only on condition that Bulgaria undertook responsibility for governing Ireland; and when Lloyd George asked if women in Bulgaria had the vote, Stamboliĭski amused his host by answering, *No, thank God!* The jesting over Macedonia masked the important point that Stamboliĭski had asked, in vain, for Britain to press the League of Nations to protect the Bulgarian minority in the area. More successfully Stamboliĭski secured Lloyd George's support for Bulgaria's bid to be admitted to the League itself.

Stamboliĭski's visit to Britain included more than political discussions and nor was it confined to London. Stamboliĭski's excursions into the provinces had been arranged by his unofficial host, the veteran *Times* Balkan journalist James Bourchier. The excursions included a visit to the University of Cambridge's School of Agriculture, to the country estate of Lord Carnarvon, an enthusiastic pig breeder who was soon to become an international celebrity after excavating Tutankhamun's tomb, to the planned new model garden city of Letchworth which Stamboliĭski thought might provide a pattern for future development in Bulgaria, and, at Stamboliĭski's own request, to a British prison, in this case Wandsworth in London. The industrial centres visited included Birmingham, Liverpool, Glasgow, where the party attended a performance by the music hall artist, Harry Lauder, and Manchester. In the latter Stamboliĭski saw the famous Ship Canal which gave him the idea that the Maritsa might be canalised from Adrianople to Dedeagach, but when he mentioned the idea to Lloyd George it was decided that the proposal had not been well thought out. Back in London more sedate tasks included the laying of a wreath on Gladstone's grave and an address to the London Chamber of Commerce.

After leaving Britain Stamboliĭski went to France but though he had discussions with a number of leading figures they were mainly formal and with little real content. Again, some time was spent in touring the country. After the signing of the treaty in 1919 Stamboliĭski had been greatly moved by a three-day visit to the battlefields of the First World War – *Three days in the land of the dead and they have made me forget my three years in prison*,[6] he said. Agriculture featured highly in the 1920 itinerary with a trip to the vineyards and farms of Provence. There was time for sight-seeing in Arles, Avignon and Nimes, as well as visits to his son and daughter, both of whom were studying in France.

From France the party travelled to Belgium where Stamboliĭski enjoyed an audience of over an hour with the king as well as a long conversation with the Belgian socialist leader Emile Van Der Velde. In addition to seeing Brussels Stamboliĭski also visited Charlerloi, Liège, Antwerp and Ghent.

There was much of substance to discuss in Stamboliĭski's next port of call, Prague. In many ways the new Czechoslovakia was the favoured child of the 1919 peace settlement: its twin founders, Tomáš Masaryk and Eduard Beneš, were widely respected, and it was democratic, relatively stable and resolutely pro-Allied. However, Masaryk and Beneš were deep in negotiations with Romania and Yugoslavia. The three states, with strong French encouragement, were constructing the Little Entente, a pro-treaty grouping in which defeated Bulgaria would hardly be welcome. Stamboliĭski found a much more sympathetic listener in Antonín Švehla. A man of great ability, he was one of the most influential of Europe's peasant leaders and, as head of the country's Agrarian Party, was to exercise enormous political power in inter-war Czechoslovakia. Stamboliĭski and Švehla agreed that Europe's best defence against bolshevism was a united agrarian movement which would form the basis for an eventual agrarian federation in central Europe and the Balkans. Švehla gave full support to Stamboliĭski's suggestion that they should found a Green International as a counter to the Red variety on offer from Moscow.

After Czechoslovakia Stamboliĭski moved on to Poland where he was received by Marshal Piłsudski who only six months before had seen off the Red Army outside the gates of Warsaw. As in Prague, however, negotiations over the projected Little Entente, for which Poland was then a candidate, preoccupied the leader of the government and for Stamboliĭski meetings with Piłsudski were little more than ceremonial. Of much greater value were his meetings with the leader of Poland's powerful peasant movement, the charismatic Wincenty Witos. Witos insisted on appearing in parliament in peasant clothes and disdained the haute bourgeois attitudes and habits of established politicians. The two were temperamentally akin and, not surprisingly, Witos gave full support to the idea of a Green International.

Stamboliĭski's final port of call was Bucharest. Here he pressed for support for Bulgaria's case over Article 48 but differences over the Dobrudja, together with the negotiations over the Little Entente, meant that little of substance was achieved.

The tour may not have achieved all its objectives but its outcome was by no means entirely negative. Stamboliĭski himself believed that he had brought Bulgaria in from the cold. He told the sŭbranie, *We have broken the ring of calumnies, falsehoods and intrigues with which our unhappy country has for a long time been blackened and stifled.*[7] Relations with Britain, or certainly with Lloyd George, were warmer and the latter was as good as his word when it came to supporting Bulgaria's application to join the League of Nations. Thanks in part to British support in 1921 Bulgaria became the first defeated state to be allowed into the new organisation. The Green International, too, became a reality. In the spring of 1921 the 'International Agrarian Bureau' invited membership from the Czechoslovak, Polish, Bulgarian and Serbian peasant parties. However, it failed to realise the potential which Stamboliĭski, Švehla and Witos saw in it. It never worked out a common programme and the individual member parties had differing objectives and fears: the Poles were more anti-Russian than the others whilst the Czechs saw it as vehicle for pan-slavism. Outside the original four the Romanians feared its predominantly Slav complexion, and the Croat Peasant Party, one of the most powerful in the region, would not join because it did not advocate independence for Croatia.

Whilst its leader had been touring Europe the BANU had continued to reconstruct Bulgaria. The objective was to create a new society built on agrarian principles. In some areas this coincided and in some it conflicted with the terms of the treaty. That those terms would be observed was the responsibility of the Allied control commission on disarmament which was backed by the presence of occupation forces which were to remain in Bulgaria until 1928.

> We have broken the ring of calumnies, falsehoods and intrigues with which our unhappy country has for a long time been blackened and stifled.
>
> STAMBOLIĬSKI

The Allies had little complaint to make over the BANU's programme for land redistribution. As there were few large landowners in Bulgaria – most of those that had existed had been in the now-alienated Dobrudja – there was no class interest which the Allies might see as threatened. If, as was the case, the most prominent victims were the monarchy and the Bulgarian Orthodox Church, few tears would be shed in London, Paris or Rome.

For the agrarians the military clauses of Neuilly presented no problems. Stamboliĭski and his followers were more than willing to strip down the army to the bare minimum dictated at Neuilly, but in the event they went even further and under their rule the number of men in uniform was below the limit set by the peace treaty. In November 1920, whilst Stamboliĭski was still abroad, the Bulgarian parliament removed control of the armed forces from the monarch; it was placed in civilian hands, as were a number of senior posts in the ministry of war traditionally held by army officers.

A more interesting situation arose over the Compulsory Labour Service (CLS). Agrarian ideology insisted that property should belong to those who worked it; it was the labour invested in a property that made it useful and gave the worker/ owner a personal stake in it. The Compulsory Labour Service, introduced in June 1920, applied this principle to the whole of the state and society. To make everyone in the country work for the country would give them all a stake in and a commitment to the new, agrarian Bulgaria. The preamble to the law stated that its intent was, 'To stimulate in all citizens, irrespective of their social and material condition, devotion to public things and love for physical labour' and 'To elevate the people morally and economically by cultivating among the citizens the sentiment of duty to themselves and society, and by teaching them rational methods of national economy.'[8] The logo on the uniform the 'trudovaks', or members of the CLS, was 'By Labour for Bulgaria'.

The law stated that all males of 20 and over must serve up to a year and all females over 16 up to six months as 'trudovaks', though Muslim women were to be exempt. The most important function of the new labour force was to repair and extend the country's infrastructure, bringing roads, improved irrigation and better public buildings, especially schools, to rural communities. Other work included planting trees and flower beds, and at least one archaeological expedition which found an important tomb. One starry-eyed observer reported that, 'In many instances this work of state service was regarded as one long picnic,' and that in Sofia, which was usually neglected by the agrarians, 'The University and school buildings were immaculate, and they had been cleaned by their respective students and pupils'. All this, together with cataloguing and repairing books, had been done under the CLS.[9] Another enthusiast noted that the first mobilisation, which was for a week only, 'contrary to expectations ... was welcomed with enthusiasm, songs, and merrymaking'.[10] There were others who looked through less rosy spectacles. For many wealthy Bulgarians the notion that their offspring should have to spend a month or more each year rubbing shoulders with the peasant masses and performing menial work was abhorrent. They latched onto concerns felt in the Allied control commission. These had been aroused because it was feared the CLS was a device for evading the limitations on Bulgaria's armed forces, fears increased by the facts that the CLS was organised on military-looking lines, wore uniforms, was a form of conscription and was initially headed by a retired general. The control commission stepped in and told the government that the CLS was an infringement of the disarmament clauses of the treaty. Stamboliĭski appealed to the council of ambassadors in Paris but the latter refused to overrule the commission. A compromise was eventually reached in October 1921.

The Stamboliĭski government had also been compelled to modify the grain consortium. Introduced in November 1919, this was an excellent example of the BANU's belief in cooperation. Three major banks combined to finance the consortium which was given a monopoly over the export of grain and which was to establish collection points, or 'centrals', to purchase grain from the peasants; where the centrals had been established private trade in grain became illegal. The consortium was to store the grain until world prices justified its sale. The profits made by the consortium were to be divided between the banks and a new organisation which was to finance agricultural improvement. The consortium succeeded in eliminating speculation in grain but it incurred the wrath of the private dealers who turned to the reparations commission for help. It obliged them by declaring that the consortium gave Bulgaria an unfair advantage in grain exporting and in 1921 the government was forced to abandon the scheme.

8

Reparations and Foreign Policy

Of all the impositions imposed by the Treaty of Neuilly on the freedom of action of the Bulgarian government none was more restricting than the need to pay reparations. The reparations commission which was to supervise payment had representatives from Britain, France and Italy. There was also a Bulgarian commissioner who could attend when invited but could not vote. The commission set its own rules and procedures and appointed its own employees and agents. The commission was to draw up a list of taxes and revenues which would cover reparations and the list could be expanded if necessary. The commission could also take over the collection of those taxes if it thought they were being improperly or inefficiently collected; in fact the commission could, if the Bulgarian government agreed, take over the management of any tax even if there had been no default. Bulgaria was to pay for the commission.

The reparations burden was heavy. It was almost a quarter of the entire national wealth and the proposed annual payment of 105 million gold francs was 55 per cent of the state budget, and this at a time when the minister of finance had estimated that taxation had reached its limit. The burden was made heavier by inflation in Bulgaria with the lev falling sevenfold between 1919 and 1923; the debt was set in gold francs so as the Bulgarian currency declined in value the number of leva needed to meet the debt rose.

This inflation had several causes. The Dobrudja and Thrace were important areas for the production respectively of grain and tobacco, both of which had been important items in Bulgaria's exports and therefore in earning it foreign currency. During the First World War Bulgaria's trading links with the west had been cut but tobacco sales to Switzerland, the Netherlands, Germany and Austria-Hungary had soared; in 1909 tobacco had accounted for 9.9 per cent of the value of Bulgarian exports; in 1917 the figure was 70 per cent. With the loss of Thrace Bulgaria would not be in a position to resume former export levels even if the economies in its former markets revived. Furthermore, immediately after the war the Allies imposed a temporary blockade around Bulgaria which strangled trade.

The war had meant a huge increase in government spending and at the same time a significant fall in tax revenues, caused by the dislocation of non-military production in the towns and by the requisitioning of crops and animals in the countryside. The end of the war meant that a gradual return to peacetime economic activity was possible, but it did not mean an end to high levels of government spending.

Although the sums expended on the army fell, those needed for welfare purposes increased. There was unemployment in the towns and a huge extra burden was created by the refugees. The delegation to Neuilly had reported that there were 300,000 of them from Macedonia, 160,000 from Thrace and 40,000 from the Dobrudja. There were an estimated 20,000

Armenians and 30,000 White Russians, the remnants of General Wrangel's defeated army, were soon to arrive. At the end of 1920 official figures recorded 175,192 registered refugee families which would make a total of around 750,000.

Reparations were bitterly resented by the Bulgarians. They believed that the requirement, albeit temporary, to deliver railway equipment, animals and coal to its neighbours had hobbled Bulgaria's economy and therefore made it more difficult to pay reparations. And there was deep resentment not only at the cost of the reparations commission but also at the lifestyle its employees enjoyed. The commission, said one observer, constituted 'a heavy financial burden on an almost ruined country, and the presence of many foreigners, who seem to have little to do and a great deal of money to spend, who occupy the best houses and command the use of a host of motor cars, is calculated to embitter the population... . The fact that a typist in the Allied Commission receives the equivalent of two and a half times the salary of a Cabinet Minister speaks for itself.'[1] And this in a society which was basically egalitarian and which had neither the experience of or the taste for small groups of ostentatiously wealthy individuals, particularly those living the high life at the cost of the hard-pressed Bulgarian taxpayer.

By 1921 it was clear that Bulgaria was in no position to make the first payment of its reparations bill and Stamboliĭski secured a postponement until March 1923. Early in 1923 the French and the Italians had become more hawkish. The French had occupied the Ruhr because of German failures to deliver full reparations, and the Italians, previous supporters of Bulgaria's moratorium, were angered by Stamboliĭski's attempts to improve relations with Rome's enemy, Yugoslavia. The Bulgarians again insisted that they could not pay the

105 million gold francs demanded as the first payment, and the reparations commission therefore authorised Romania, Greece and Yugoslavia to seize Bulgarian customs posts and gave permission for Yugoslavia to occupy the mines in Pernik. Feeling as to these proposals may be gauged by the fact that at the time several ex-ministers were being tried by the High Court in Sofia for their acquiescence in the terms of a German loan of 1914, 'which did not involve anything like as complete a surrender of internal control as is now demanded by the reparation commission'.[2] In fact the Yugoslavs declined to act because they did not wish to endanger the burgeoning rapprochement with Bulgaria which Stamboliĭski was engineering. Romania and Greece could do nothing without Yugoslavia and the Bulgarians seized the initiative, telling the reparations commission once again that they could not pay. The log-jam broke. In March 1923 a new agreement was signed which greatly eased the burdens laid on Bulgaria. The reparations debt was to be divided into two sections, the first of 550 million gold francs was to be paid over 60 years, and payment of the remaining 1,700 million gold francs was not to begin until 1953. The first payment on the 550 million gold francs was to be of five rather than the original 105 million gold francs, and the sum was to rise gradually thereafter until the liquidation of this debt in 1983. But even after this reduction the payments by the end of the 1920s were estimated to account for a quarter of the budget. When reparations were abandoned in 1932 Bulgaria had paid 40 million gold francs.

ooooo

Reparations were inextricably bound in with foreign policy. Stamboliĭski shared the general opinion in Bulgaria that the

loss of Thrace was one of the reasons for Bulgaria's economic difficulties. In 1922 *L'Echo de Bulgarie* reported that
he believed that for Bulgaria the loss of Thrace was 'like a
slip knot round the neck, which does not necessarily entail
death, but, undoubtedly, will interfere with normal respira-
tion. He understands that Bulgaria should be punished but
not that this punishment should last for ever. He cites the
heavy storms that have recently taken place on the Black Sea
and the freezing up of the Danube as the work of destiny to
show the world that they have not got sufficient access to the
open sea.'[3]

The reasons for this were not hard to find. Although they
could not make a claim to ethnic domination there the area
was the preferred economic outlet for Bulgaria, giving access to
the open sea of the Aegean thus relieving Bulgaria of depend-
ence on the politically sensitive Straits. The Allies responded
that the treaty would ensure that in future the Straits would
remain open. Even if that were the case, however, a port on
the Aegean would shorten the journey from Bulgaria to the
markets of western Europe by hundreds of miles, and would
allow Bulgarian tobacco easy access to the market. There was
also the strategic argument that to deny Bulgaria access to the
Mediterranean would force it back on the Danube and thus
to look to central rather than western Europe.

The treaty had allowed Bulgaria economic access to the
Aegean but had not suggested how this might be achieved.
In August 1920 the Allies had declared Dedeagach a port of
international interest and gave Bulgaria the right to apply to
the League for the appointment of a commissioner to ensure
the proper carrying out of the agreements connected with that
port. It was not an attractive proposition. Like Porto Lagos,
the only other port under consideration, it was far from Sofia

and could be reached only via the meandering and exposed Maritsa valley, and it had the further disadvantage that it had no deep-water docking facilities and was no more than a shallow-water, open roadstead. The most suitable outlet was Kavalla and soon after the signature of the Treaty of Neuilly the Greek prime minister, Venizelos, had offered Bulgaria the use of this port with a railway to be built from there through the Struma valley to the Sofia-Salonica line. But who would pay for such a line? Even if it could have afforded to do so Bulgaria would not; the line would run through Greek territory and therefore be at the mercy of the Greeks; and the Greeks were hardly likely to take out their wallets to further the interests of a political and economic rival.

Western Thrace was initially placed under Allied control. A month after the signing of the treaty General Franchet d'Esperey began ensuring that all Bulgarian officials left the area. He took command and was assisted by an administrative bureau appointed by himself and by a superior administrative council composed of all various local nationalities except the Bulgarians; it was assumed they would all have left. This arrangement – local officials under a foreign governor – had before the First World War been regarded as the classic solution to Balkan problems. In 1919 it was one which the Bulgarians could tolerate because it offered the possibility that the area could in the future be reassigned.

Stamboliĭski certainly placed his hopes in this eventuality. What he feared was that Thrace might be handed to Greece. Shortly after the war he had asked a British journalist what were the intentions of Britain with regard to Thrace, adding as an aside, *As long as it is not given to Greece*.[4] It was. In the late spring and early summer of 1920 conferences at St Remo and Bologna decided that the French forces should withdraw and that western Thrace be handed to Greece; this was confirmed in Article 84 of the Treaty of Sèvres. Despite fierce resistance from the local Muslims and Bulgarians, Greek troops and officials took control of the area. Stamboliĭski was not entirely downhearted. He still believed that if Bulgaria proved its good intent and faithfully observed the Neuilly rules the Allies would grant access to the Aegean and, eventually realising that Greek-Bulgarian mutual suspicion made the situation untenable, would restore western Thrace to Bulgaria. In the meantime he continued to press for the corridor to the Aegean which Neuilly had guaranteed to Bulgaria.

An interim solution, which would serve international interests as well as those of Bulgaria, would be to make western Thrace an autonomous province under the protection of the League. The chance to press this solution came when Greek defeats in Asia Minor and further changes of leader in Athens dictated a revision of the now defunct Treaty of Sèvres. Bulgaria had hardly been in a position to involve itself in the Greek-Turkish dispute and Stamboliĭski had played the role of interested but uninvolved observer skilfully and wisely. But he could not afford to miss the opportunity which was offered when the conference to redesign Sèvres opened in Lausanne in the second half of 1922.

The Bulgarian government had taken some encouragement from indications that British attitudes were changing in view of the Greek defeat in Asia Minor. Lloyd George was now reported to be worrying over Turkish nationalist demands which could soon stretch to Constantinople. In these circumstances an enfeebled Greece might not be the best custodian of western Thrace. Initially the Bulgarians, backed by Russia, fell back on their interim solution and pressed for the area to be made autonomous under the aegis of the League. The other Balkan states, however, had enough historical memory to recall the Eastern Rumelian case and the idea was dropped. In response the Greeks offered transit rights over Greek territory and a perpetual lease on Dedeagach or a Bulgarian free zone in Salonica. This the Bulgarians would not accept. Early in 1923, however, the Greek position weakened further. Not only had its armies in Asia Minor been defeated but a growing rapprochement between Bulgaria and Yugoslavia raised the fears that the two states might 'run down' to Salonica and into Thrace respectively. Venizelos therefore offered to cede a strip of territory running down to Dedeagach in return for Bulgaria's ceding an equivalent amount of territory in the west. Stamboliĭski's administration was toppled whilst these discussions were in progress and despite constant efforts subsequent Bulgarian diplomacy never did secure implementation of Article 48.

Whilst pressing his case over Thrace and Article 48 Stamboliĭski had also been doing his utmost to improve relations with Yugoslavia, and by the end of 1922 had made considerable progress. The rapprochement with Yugoslavia was central to Stamboliĭski's foreign policy objectives. Before 1913 he had devoted relatively little time and thought to foreign policy. He had grand strategic designs, principally that of a Balkan agrarian federation, but he had little experience of or interest in the tactical manoeuvring which was the everyday task of the diplomat. As he himself admitted, one of the purposes of his 1920 tour of Europe was to *school himself in diplomacy.*[5] Stamboliĭski proved to be an adept pupil as his handling of the Aegean question had shown.

He was perhaps lucky in that the peace settlement urged Bulgaria to follow policies of which he approved. The peacemakers wanted a stable Balkans. So did Stamboliĭski. Stability in the Balkans demanded good relations between Bulgaria and its neighbours. This Stamboliĭski was keen to bring about, even at the cost of sacrificing some of Bulgaria's traditional national aspirations. Therein lay the rub. There were many Bulgarians who were not prepared for that sacrifice.

Stamboliĭski had set out his general strategy in *The Principles of the BANU*, written whilst he was still in prison: *The Agrarian Union is for lasting, peaceful and neighbourly relations between Bulgaria and the surrounding states. It is against any provocation on [Bulgaria's (sic)] part tending towards armed conflict. Its efforts are directed at strengthening good relations by the union of Bulgaria with the other Balkan states on a federative basis.*[6]

Soon after the war he reiterated his peaceful intentions. *The aim of the present Government is to prove to our neighbours and the victorious States that in Bulgaria there is and there will be no conspiracy against any one. We will disturb the tranquillity of nobody.*[7] In 1921 he allowed himself to indulge in what in retrospect must seem a flight of fancy: *The Balkan nations today have the greatest need for peace and harmony. The wars have visited upon these peoples new injustices but they have also created the conditions in which those injustices might be remedied. In all the Balkan states the surge for rule by the people has swelled and is continuing to swell. That is a great pledge for the immediate future of our world. We earnestly hope that the entire developed world will assist these peoples' efforts to create a lasting peace amongst themselves. What is most needed for the creation of such a lasting peace in the Balkans? What is needed is quite simple; it is: 1. The peoples of the contested areas be allowed to determine their own fate. 2. The minority rights written into the peace treaties be honoured fully under international control. 3. All*

Balkan nations be granted secure and appropriate access to the open sea. Implement these three points and the Balkans will progress to that lasting and secure peace which will soon push all the nations inhabiting it in the direction of culture and progress and will open a wide field for the creation of something akin to the United States of America which must be the ideal of every person in the Balkans.[8]

Nevertheless, Bulgaria's neighbours remained suspicious, but usually without cause. In 1921 Yugoslavia, Romania and Greece protested to Bulgaria and to the supreme council in Paris at incursions from Bulgaria and said the Bulgarian government had not done enough to implement the disarmament clauses. The Bulgarians replied that they would gladly join a commission of enquiry into the allegations. Romania was the only state to respond and a joint commission decided that the problems were caused mainly by smugglers and the laxity of customs officials.[9]

Nevertheless, the *comitadjis*, the irregular armed bands which had been so prominent before the Balkan wars, remained a problem. The Yugoslavs and the Greeks complained regularly that these groups were infiltrating their territory to commit sabotage or other illegal acts. But Bulgaria also suffered from incursions and Stamboliĭski's government argued that if Belgrade and Athens were prepared to cooperate with Sofia the problem could be solved. The activities of the *comitadjis* showed that the Macedonian problem which had so long bedevilled internal Bulgarian politics and complicated relations between Bulgaria and its neighbours was still active.

Macedonia had been ignored in the Treaty of Neuilly because it had been assigned to Yugoslavia. Stamboliĭski made little of this. Indeed, he went further. In September

1921 he stated baldly, *Bulgaria disinterests herself from Macedonia.*[10] It was the first time since the Treaty of Berlin that a Bulgarian leader had dared say such a thing. Yet it was crucial to the success both of his short term tactics and long term strategy. A Balkan federation was impossible without good relations between Bulgaria and Yugoslavia; good relations between Bulgaria and Yugoslavia would be impossible unless the Macedonian issue was resolved. And the Macedonian issue would not be resolved as long as the *comitadjis'* incursions continued.

Stopping the incursions would not be easy. The frontier was long and difficult to monitor and the Bulgarian army was of insufficient strength to carry out the task. Many of the incursions were launched from Petrich near where the Bulgarian, Greek and Yugoslav frontiers met. Here a faction of IMRO had established a virtual state within the state which seemed beyond Sofia's control. Stamboliĭski did what he could to contain the Macedonians, purging their supporters from the army and the frontier guards, but their response was to assassinate the minister of war and the chief of police in the Petrich region. The Yugoslavs were not convinced by Bulgarian assurances that the Sofia regime had nothing to do with the terrorists and in 1922 became more assertive over Macedonia. In July Yugoslavia, Romania and Greece warned Bulgaria that if it did not put its house in order they would intervene and do it themselves; Bulgaria was again facing the coalition which had inflicted the disastrous defeat of 1913. Stamboliĭski responded by proposing a joint Yugoslav-Bulgarian frontier force and immediately appealed to the League for an investigation into the Macedonian situation. This prevented any further local action by the three neighbouring states and the League's judgement was a victory for

Stamboliĭski; it recommended discussions on the basis of Stamboliĭski's suggestion of a joint frontier force.

The League's decision made it possible, at last, for Stamboliĭski to visit Belgrade. Speaking there in November 1922 he denounced the Macedonian extremists as the origin of Bulgaria's misfortunes, including the Second Balkan War. Relations with Yugoslavia improved rapidly and in March 1923 Stamboliĭski and the Yugoslav premier, Pašić, signed the Niš convention pledging themselves to a joint campaign against the terrorists. In April Stamboliĭski acted on the agreement. All terrorist organisations were banned, their publications shut down and many of their leaders interned in camps in eastern Bulgaria.

However, Stamboliĭski's victory over the Macedonian extremists was to be short-lived.

Aleksandŭr Stamboliĭski (1879–1923), the dominant figure in the Bulgarian Agrarian National Union; prime minister 1919–23.

III

The Legacy

9

The Fall of Stamboliĭski

Nadezhda Stanciov wrote in December 1919 of her admiration for her boss, 'I really like him very much and I have a lot of confidence in him, if Bulgaria only will let him work in peace.'[1] It didn't. On 9 June 1923 an efficiently organised coup deposed the BANU government. Stamboliĭski was at the time at his home in Slavovitsa. He went into hiding but was discovered on 14 June, tortured, mutilated and finally beheaded; it was said that his head was sent to Sofia in a biscuit tin.

The coup had been engineered by an alliance of disgruntled army officers, leaders of the old parliamentary parties and Macedonian extremists. It was almost certainly carried out with the knowledge of the king, though it is unlikely that he would have approved of the excesses committed during it. There was relatively little resistance, most of it being concentrated in the Pleven area where agrarianism had always been strong and where the local communists, until ordered by the party leadership to cease doing so, had supported the agrarians.

Stamboliĭski's government did not fall because it had failed to enact social reform. Given its financial difficulties and the restraints imposed by the treaty its achievements in this sector were considerable. The eight-hour day was introduced, as was a progressive income tax, enactments which benefited the urban as well as the rural masses. The latter were also the main focus of agrarian attention. In June 1920 legislation had been introduced to set up a state land fund into which would be paid property held in excess of 30 hectares, though a more generous allowance was given to large families and in some areas of unproductive land; absentee landlords were to retain no more than four hectares. These rulings were to apply to crown properties and, after 1921, to monastic lands not worked by monks themselves. Land brought into the fund was to be redistributed to peasants whose properties were insufficient for the maintenance of their families. Dispossessed owners were to be compensated in government bonds. This was classic agrarian thinking: the law sought to protect only private property used directly by its owners to provide for their immediate family. The intention had been to redistribute around a quarter of a million hectares but when the BANU government was deposed less than half that area had passed through the hands of the state land fund. This was not entirely surprising in a society where there were few large landowners to dispossess and relatively few peasants who did not have enough land to maintain their families.

Land redistribution was not the only way in which Stamboliĭski hoped to enhance the welfare of the peasant. There were energetic measures to promote commassation, the bringing together into one compact holding of strips

> 'What they did is abominable!'
>
> **KING BORIS ON THE MURDER OF STAMBOLIĬSKI**[2]

held scattered about the village fields or even in other villages. Peasants were encouraged, though never compelled, to join cooperatives which the government favoured whenever the watchful Allies would allow them to do so. The cooperative principle was successfully extended to the urban sector with new large apartment blocks, the construction of which was financed by cooperatives but where the individual flats were privately owned. The government was also keen to promote crop diversification and more selective breeding of animals, the responsibility for doing this being given to the agricultural advisors who had existed before 1920 but who were now given more prominence and prestige. Stamboliĭski hoped to bring to every village in Bulgaria the modern amenities of the cinema and the radio, whilst great efforts were made to improve the infrastructure of the countryside. To this end roads were built, or straightened, bridges were constructed or repaired, and the telegraph and telephone network extended. Much of the work these projects demanded was provided via the CLS. Building schools was a high priority. Education was a key factor in agrarian policy and Stamboliĭski's government was responsible for the building of 300 new primary and 800 new secondary schools; the high number of the latter was a consequence of the government's decision to make secondary schooling compulsory up to the age of 14. Education was to be different in quality as well as quantity. The agrarians hoped to eradicate the nationalism which had dominated much of teaching before 1920, and the time allotted to practical subjects, especially agriculture, was to be extended. At the tertiary level the government founded a higher institute for forestry, and established a veterinary faculty in Sofia University. A radical feature of the educational reforms was the application of agrarian democracy to primary schools where older parties did, sizeable cadres of educated or experienced administrators. Some ministers were scarcely able to cope with the demands of running a department, and their short-comings were all the more apparent during Stamboliĭski's fre-quent and sometimes prolonged journeyings abroad.

That the agrarians were left in the lurch by most com-munists in June 1923 was hardly surprising. The BCP still regarded the agrarians as a petit bourgeois phenomenon, and more importantly, the communists were still smarting at the wounds the BANU-dominated government had inflicted on them in 1919 and 1920. The communists' decision to leave the agrarian regime to its fate had been taken by party leaders in Sofia. Moscow then decided they had been wrong and told them to rectify the situation. The result was an ill-prepared communist rebellion in September 1923 which was crushed with ease and severity.

The working class and its leaders were not the only section of the urban population which shed few tears at the removal of the Stamboliĭski government. The agrarians had never had great respect for certain sections of the professions. Teachers, engineers and others who brought benefit to the masses they could appreciate, but soldiers and lawyers they could not. The Treaty of Neuilly had solved the question of the former but the latter were left to the not too tender mercies of the BANU government. The peasants had frequently had cause to resent the lawyers who charged high fees in litigation over family affairs and above all in the boundary disputes which were a perennial feature of land farmed in separate strips. Stamboliĭski's government therefore created new local courts which would be given power to decide on these disputes, and in which the judges were to be elected by the local peasantry. At a higher level, one of the BANU's first acts in coming to power was to ban lawyers from high office and to make it illegal for them to be elected to parliament or local councils.

The lawyers were not the only professional group to resent agrarian rule. The officer corps was another obvious example, not least because many of its members were now unemployed and impoverished. But teachers, too, had cause for complaint. Shortly after coming to power Stamboliĭski had purged the profession of many with communist sympathies. Teachers also resented the fact that their posts were to be subject to four-yearly review. University teachers were few in number but they exercised considerable influence and they were displeased when the new government attempted to remove the numerous socialists from their profession; this they saw as unwarrantable interference in the internal affairs of the university. Doctors and nurses, meanwhile, were unhappy at plans to force many of them to practise in remote country areas. The Church disliked the redistribution of monastic property, the enforced removal of the Holy Synod from Sofia to the monastery at Rila, and disapproved of what was generally believed to be Stamboliĭski's relaxed attitude towards sexual morality.

There were many city dwellers outside the professions who were undisturbed by these new restrictions, but there were very few who did not bitterly resent the application of agrarian ideas on the redistribution of property to the urban context. There was a severe housing shortage in many towns because of the influx of refugees and because home building had been minimal during the war. The Stamboliĭski government ruled that each family be restricted to two rooms and a kitchen, with larger families having more accommodation. The legislation was also to apply to office space and was to be enforced by government inspectors. In the towns they became perhaps the most hated aspect of agrarian rule. Townspeople also resented the agrarians' stated preference for the countryside. It was not just that Stamboliĭski could liken Sofia to Sodom and Gomorrah, surely one of history's grossest exaggerations, but also that the urban population felt that they were over-taxed and that insufficient government spending was devoted to the towns which became increasingly grubby and unkempt.

The agrarians did much to further alienate the old parliamentary parties. Until 1922 they suffered under some restraints as a result of the stage of siege imposed by Stamboliĭski during the urban unrest of 1919–20, but their press was still lively and many of their leaders had close ties with the Allies. With the lifting of the state of siege the old parties expanded their activities, both in their press and in public meetings. They were growing increasingly concerned at Stamboliĭski's long term objectives, fearing he might be moving towards the establishment of a one-party system. They saw confirmation of their fears in the creation of the Orange Guard which they believed to be an attempt to replace the existing police with an agrarian party force. There were other measures by which, the old parties thought, the agrarians were replacing the established machinery of government with BANU institutions. Legislative proposals, for example, were generally sent for review not to parliament or to the crown as the constitution required, but to the BANU's permanent council. At a lower level, in the process of land redistribution, it was not the existing local government apparatus which was given the task of handing land to the needy peasants, but the local BANU associations, the *druzhbi*, and the appointment of teachers and other officials by peasant committees rather than by the established organs of local government was seen as another intrusion of the party into the civil service. More alarming for the older parties was what seemed to be a government offensive against them. Few had cavilled when the sŭbranie decided to put those members of the Radoslavov government still in the country on trial, but in November 1922 it was decided to begin proceedings against the members of the Danev, Geshov and Malinov cabinets. It seemed that Stamboliĭski was preparing to liquidate his major bourgeois opponents. Stamboliĭski's tinkering with the constitution also fuelled the fears of the old parties. They were hardly ones to raise their eyebrows when he manufactured his parliamentary majority in 1920 but they were concerned at his abolition of PR in 1923, shortly before the elections due that year.

Their fear of constitutional change had prompted the leaders of the old parliamentary parties to form the Constitutional Bloc in 1922. The Bloc then organised three major rallies to defend the existing political system. The rallies were to begin in Tŭrnovo, the home of Bulgarian constitutionalism, and to end with a march on Sofia; after Rome in 1922 marching on capitals was in vogue. When their train approached Tŭrnovo in September for the first rally some of the leaders of the Bloc were attacked and probably saved from serious physical harm only by the action of Raĭko Daskalov, the erstwhile leader of the Radomir rebellion, who was also on the train. For a short period the threatened party leaders were locked up in Shumen jail for their own safety. Meanwhile, the Orange Guard took over in Tŭrnovo and the government banned public meetings.

As the leaders of the Bloc had feared, the ending of PR, plus the exercise of some governmental influence at the polls, produced a massive majority for the BANU in the elections of April 1923; it had 212 seats to the BCP's 16 and the Bloc's

15. The opposition's worst fears were now confirmed. After the elections the government purged the administration of more opponents and at meetings BANU members swore to lay down their lives for the party. Stamboliĭski himself heightened the expectation of decisive intervention by appearing at an Orange Guard parade seated upon a white charger. Even if Stamboliĭski did not declare for a new constitution and make himself dictator of an agrarian republic, many in the old parties feared that the more radical elements in his party would remove him and do it themselves. In fact, Stamboliĭski had no taste for such a change, basically because he did not think it necessary; the peasant masses, he believed, would always be faithful to the BANU which therefore did not need to replace the existing system.

Of this the opposition leaders were not convinced. Nor were they confident that their Constitutional Bloc would prove strong enough to defend itself against extremist radical designs. Even before the elections its leaders had linked themselves with the National Alliance, an elitist association of professionals and members of the Military League. The Military League dated back to before the First World War and by the early 1920s it was headed by General Protogerov who had organised the defence of Sofia against the Radomir rebels in 1919, and who in 1921 had attempted to construct an anti-government conspiracy. He failed because the Democratic Party, the most radical and respected of the old parties, had refused to join in. By 1923 the Democrats' fears of the BANU's intentions had so increased that they no longer wished to stand aside. They joined a plot hatched that year by the Military League, the National Alliance, IMRO and a few Social Democrats. The two most important elements in the plot were the Military League and IMRO. The former brought the training and discipline of the officer corps whilst the latter added the ruthlessness of the terrorist. Protogerov himself was a Macedonian and the association of the Constitutional Bloc with the Military League therefore linked the old parties to the most powerful of all the discontented elements in Stamboliĭski's Bulgaria, the Macedonians.

By declaring Bulgaria no longer had an interest in Macedonia Stamboliĭski was acting in response to the Treaty of Neuilly and through agrarian conviction. It was the search for national reunification through military means, he argued, that had forced Bulgaria into the hands of manipulative foreign sponsors, had brought about vast and crippling expenditure on the army and the monarchy, and which had created the officer corps as a divisive and domineering caste in an egalitarian society. Yet however much the decision on Macedonia conformed to agrarian ideology it was a huge gamble. For most Bulgarians, including the peasants, Macedonia remained part of Bulgaria's legitimate national aspirations, even if repossession of it was temporarily out of the question. Furthermore, the arrival of tens of thousands of destitute and embittered Bulgarians from Macedonia only added to the strength of feeling on the issue.

The ruthlessness of the Macedonian extremists had been amply proven. In October 1921 they assassinated Aleksandŭr Dimitrov, the minister of war and a close ally and friend of Stamboliĭski; in February 1923 they tried to kill Stamboliĭski himself. A few month's earlier the Metropolitan of Sofia had suggested privately to Stamboliĭski that the government pay 50 million leva to the extremists to cease their activities; Stamboliĭski's response had been, *With your plan, My Lord, you would send the government to hell.*[3] The violence was directed not merely against their opponents within the administration. There were fierce feuds between the varying Macedonian factions; in October 1922 one IMRO unit occupied the town of Nevrokop in an attempt to liquidate a rival group. Such actions were dangerous because they might give the Allies or Bulgaria's neighbours the impression that the Bulgarian government was not in control of the country, and that would seriously weaken Stamboliĭski's efforts to improve relations with the surrounding states. Macedonian hostility reached fever pitch after the Niš agreement and the repressive measures which it precipitated. IMRO said it would not regard the agreement's terms as binding and would do 'its sacred duty to frustrate them'.[4] As proof of its intent it not only resumed terrorist activities in Yugoslavia but also occupied the western Bulgarian town of Kyustendil. That the government used the Orange Guard rather than the army to dislodge them was, in the eyes of Stamboliĭski's opponents, another example of the BANU party machinery usurping the rightful organs of the state.

> With your plan, My Lord, you would send the government to hell.
> STAMBOLIĬSKI TO THE METROPOLITAN OF SOFIA

Despite what his enemies might allege Stamboliĭski was not lacking in national pride or feeling, though his was always a nationalism focused upon peasant democracy rather than territorial aspirations. When the Yugoslavs threatened to occupy the Pernik mines in 1923 because of the alleged underpayment of reparations, Stamboliĭski told the king that if there was an occupation he would lead the fight against it, because *a nation which does not defend its territorial integrity does not deserve to live in freedom.*[5]

The 1923 coup was an internal affair, but it was not uninfluenced by external factors. The plotters were helped by the fact that no one outside Bulgaria, with the belated and ineffectual effort of the Comintern in Moscow, was prepared to intervene to reverse it. Stamboliĭski's radical agrarian ideology excited little sympathy amongst the ruling elements in Romania, and in Yugoslavia the powerful agrarian parties were located in Slovenia and Croatia, not in Serbia which dominated the new state.

Nor did the Great Powers greatly interest themselves in happenings in Bulgaria. They had little time for a radical regime in what was still generally regarded first and foremost as a defeated state. In fact this was a short-sighted view. It was a view to some degree coloured by misinterpretations of Stamboliĭski's relations with the bolsheviks and with the Soviet Union. Some regarded him with suspicion because the communists had been his preferred option for coalition partners in 1919 and 1920, and then because he had taken support from and wanted to establish full diplomatic relations with Lenin's regime in 1922. But internally Stamboliĭski never favoured the communists. Quite the contrary; he cleared them out of the teaching profession and towards the end of his regime he announced a scheme whereby communists would be thrown out of their homes if there were too many of them in a village. And if he showed a willingness to establish diplomatic relations with Lenin's pariah state this was because that state gave Bulgaria support over Thrace, and because by that stage in Soviet Russia the anti-peasant excesses of 'war communism' were giving way to the more tolerant attitudes of the New Economic Policy.

Stamboliĭski had lost power because he had alienated all those outside his party and the peasantry who might have come to his aid. He had failed to take sufficient guard against the most determined of his opponents because he saw no need for such measures. He took little care for his personal safety, spurning the use of a bullet-proof car imported into Bulgaria by one of his colleagues, and in Switzerland he refused special protection even though the police had evidence of a Macedonian plot to assassinate him. He believed that peasant support for the BANU was so entrenched that any coup could not last more than a few weeks and that the agrarian movement was so great that it would continue in power, carried forward by its own democratic momentum. Neither he, nor any but a small number of fanatics amongst the plotters had foreseen that the coup would become so violent. Yet in the last resort it was the most violent of those conspirators, the Macedonian extremists, who had dealt the cruellest blow to the BANU and to agrarianism. The gamble of the September 1919 declaration had failed. When they captured him his tormentors sliced off 'the hands that had signed the Niš convention'.

10
From Coup to Coup (1923–34)

Once in power the architects of the June 1923 coup formed a new association, the Democratic Alliance, the main constituents of which were the National Alliance and the Military League. It was broadly split between moderates such as Andreǐ Lyapchev and those who favoured more authoritarian rule prominent amongst whom was Aleksandŭr Tsankov, a professor of economics.

Tough measures were taken immediately after the coup with large numbers of agrarians being detained and even larger numbers fleeing into exile, many of them in Yugoslavia; more were to follow in 1924 and 1925. After 1923 the BANU split. Divisions within the movement had never been far below the surface. The major division after 1923, as before, was on the question of relations with the left wing parties of the old political establishment. The two main agrarian factions were Vrabcha-1 (Sparrow-1) and Pladne-1 (Noon-1), both claiming, of course, to be the true heirs of Stamboliǐski. Vrabcha under the leadership of Dimitŭr Gichev was prepared to work with the left-wing established parties but this was rejected by Pladne which was formed amongst the agrarians in exile and in which the dominant personality was Kosta Todorov. There were also differences over foreign policy, with Gichev being willing to accept that, because cooperation with Yugoslavia seemed a lost cause, Bulgaria should revert to a revisionist attitude. Others refused to relinquish the notion of a Balkan federation. There were further differences over which foreign power Bulgaria should associate with; before collectivisation was imposed in the Soviet Union Bulgaria's traditional slavophilism made closer relations with Russia preferable for some, whilst others looked to the western European powers, or to Germany or to fascist Italy. So riven were the deposed agrarians that it has been observed that they were divided not into separate wings but into feathers.

Having neutralised the BANU the Democratic Alliance arranged for elections to be held in November; the poll produced the predictable government majority. Within the Democratic Alliance it seemed that the moderates would prevail, the government having reacted relatively calmly to the communist rising in September 1923, doing little more than enacting a defence of the realm act. The situation changed in April 1925 when the authoritarians took full control after the communists planted a bomb in Sofia's Sveta Nedelya Cathedral during a funeral service attended by the king and leading public figures. Over 130 people were killed, though the king was not amongst them. The repression which followed was more savage than anything yet seen in Bulgaria; thousands were arrested, including a number of leading agrarians; many of those arrested disappeared, some of them, according to rumour, fed into the furnaces of the central heating system in Sofia central prison, and there were a number of public executions. The main instigator of the terror was Tsankov. The Sveta Nedelya outrage also persuaded the Allies to relax temporarily the military clauses of the Treaty of Neuilly. The conference of ambassadors had already agreed to an increase of 3,000 in the army as a precaution against communism and after the April bombing they allowed an extra 10,000 to be recruited, though most of these were to be stood down by 31 May.

The Tsankovist terror horrified most Bulgarians; it also shocked the outside world. This became apparent in 1926 when the Bulgarian government approached the League of Nations for a loan to cope with the refugee problem. The government in Sofia argued that if left in their present condition the refugees would become easy prey for the communists or the terrorists. The League was persuaded and agreed to the loan, stipulating that its beneficiaries had to be Bulgarian citizens; therefore, refugees accepting money had to renounce their previous citizenship which, it was hoped, would do something to ease tension within the Balkans. It certainly helped reduce social suffering and tensions in Bulgaria itself; by the turn of the decade 100,000 refugees had been settled, many of them on land drained thanks to funds from the loan. It was another condition of the loan, however, which revealed the extent of foreign distaste for the 'White Terror' which had been imposed on Bulgaria. During the negotiations for the loan in London where most of the money was to be raised the financiers made it clear that they regarded Tsankov and his henchmen as unsavoury and their violent policies as a threat to political stability. They would only lend the money if he stepped down. In January 1926 he did so and Lyapchev became prime minister.

Lyapchev was a member of the Democratic Party. He was to be the longest serving prime minister of the inter-war period, remaining in office until June 1931. He was also a

Macedonian. Macedonia had been a problem for the Tsankov cabinet before the loan and it was to remain one for Lyap-chev's administration after it.

The extremists of IMRO continued their vendetta against the agrarians even after June 1923, and in August of that year murdered Raĭko Daskalov in Prague. The violence intensified when one particular Macedonian faction decided to create an unholy alliance with the communists who at that time were calling for the dismemberment of Yugoslavia. This precipi-tated yet another feud and led to a number of murders in the towns and cities of Bulgaria itself. It has been estimated that between 1923 and 1934 the Macedonians were responsible for over 800 murders in the country.

The Macedonians complicated Bulgaria's external as well as its domestic affairs. Incursions from the Petrich enclave continued. A particularly serious incident took place in October 1925 when an IMRO unit occupied a Greek military frontier post, killing a Greek frontier guard in the process. In retaliation a division of Greek troops occupied areas along the Greek-Bulgarian border for five days, killing 12 Bulgarians, seven of whom were civilians. It was the most serious incident of the inter-war period and it raised fears of a renewed conflict in the Balkans. The League of Nations stepped in, ordering the Greeks to withdraw. The League also set up a commission of inquiry under the British diplomat, Sir Horace Rumbold. It recommended that a convention signed in 1919 between Athens and Sofia on the voluntary exchange of populations should be implemented as soon as possible. The Greeks were ordered to pay £16,000 in com-pensation to the Bulgarians. Rumbold's commission also had interesting observations on the way in which the border in the area was controlled; frontier duties were unpopular, it was recorded, and were frequently carried out by very young soldiers or individuals of dubious character. Some of the chickens released by Neuilly's military terms were coming home to roost. The Rumbold commission had an important impact in Bulgaria. It had not treated the country like a 'defeated' state but as a fully independent country with rights equal to those which had been on the winning side in 1918. The Bulgarians could feel that they had at last emerged from their isolation; it was, in a minor fashion, their Locarno.[1]

The hope that the Macedonian Lyapchev might have more influence in this sector was one reason why he was chosen to replace Tsankov in January 1926. His appointment made little difference. In August 1926 the Yugoslav government complained once more about incursions and threatened retaliation if they did not cease. Yugoslav policy-makers were suspicious of the new Bulgarian prime minister not least because he was a Macedonian, as were a number of his ministerial colleagues; in Belgrade his administration was nicknamed 'the Macedonian government'.

In the event under Lyapchev the Macedonians, though not repressed, did not greatly expand their activities. They were to some degree bought off by being given a large number of government jobs, a fact which many Bulgarians resented, and they continued to exercise considerable influence in the army; in 1930 the whole nation was shocked by revelations of how Macedonians had tortured a soldier in order to force him to give false testimony against a senior officer opposed to them. Despite these problems both the Bulgarian and Yugoslav governments had by the end of the 1920s realised that the present situation along their border had to be changed. Bulgarian resources, partly because of the restrictions of Neuilly, were inadequate whilst Bulgaria's neighbours were armed to the

teeth. In order to improve the prospects of agreement Lyapchev arrested a number of Macedonian leaders and interned
them in camps. This reassured the Yugoslavs and in 1929 and
1930 the Pirot agreements were signed covering a number of
detailed issues concerning the frontier, such as railway connections and access to properties divided by the border. The
two governments also pledged themselves to settle amicably
all future disagreements arising over border disputes. Bulgaria
never received another note of complaint from Yugoslavia on
this issue.

After the fall of Stamboliĭski Bulgarian policy-makers continued his efforts to have Article 48 of the Treaty of Neuilly
implemented. The aspiration was to convince the world,
through the League of Nations, that the denial of Bulgaria's
access to the Aegean was an infringement of the post-war
settlement which inflicted considerable economic damage
on Bulgaria. Although the League was to be the mechanism
through which Bulgaria pursued its objective both Tsankov
and Lyapchev recognised that Bulgaria's case would be more
readily heard if Sofia had the backing of a major power. In
the 1920s it was assumed that Italy was the most appropriate
sponsor and in 1930 King Boris married the Italian Princess
Giovanna of Savoy. The association with Italy was logical.
Italy, if not a great power, was not a minor one. It was also
a victor power but one with its own revisionist desires. The
constellation of European forces also made Italy Bulgaria's
preferred backer. Britain was largely uninterested in conti-
nental affairs, Russia and Germany were out of the fold, even
after Locarno, and France was an energetic supporter of the
Little Entente of Czechoslovakia, Romania and Yugoslavia.
With Yugoslavia and Bulgaria at loggerheads over Macedonia
France would not be interested in Bulgaria's case. But Italy

would because it too, for its own largely nefarious purposes, wished to limit Yugoslav power.

Whilst gently but ineffectively pursuing implementation of Article 48 the Lyapchev administration had allowed many of the faults of the old Bulgarian political system to reappear. One problem was that few political parties seemed to have any real ideology or purpose. The agrarians had been harried from power and put under great constraint, whilst the BCP was banned in 1923. The Democratic Party still held to the principles of representative parliamentary democracy and its leader, Aleksandŭr Malinov, refused to join his party colleague Lyapchev in coalition with the likes of Tsankov. Lacking clear ideologies or even social programmes the parties became café parties, held together not by common belief but by personal ties and even more by a desire for the spoils of office. Lyapchev did make one attempt to remedy the problem by introducing the Italian fascist principle that the party winning the largest share of the votes at an election would be guaranteed a majority in the sŭbranie. This so-called quota system made matters worse rather than better because it precipitated an unseemly scramble to form blocs and alliances. This overt horse-trading brought further discredit on the political establishment. Nevertheless, the new system, introduced in time for the elections of May 1927, did provide Lyapchev with a stable parliamentary majority. In addition to introducing the quota system, Lyapchev also eased some of the controls imposed on political activity during the terror. The BCP was allowed to reappear as the Bulgarian Workers' Party (BWP) and the agrarians were allowed to combine with the Social Democrats in the elections of 1927, though they won only 11 seats.

The majority created by the elections of 1927 lasted until

those of 1931. These were unusual. They were free and open. And they were held before the formation of a new government. The parliament of 1931 brought to power a newly formed coalition, the People's Bloc, which included three agrarians, one of whom was Gichev.

A major reason for allowing an open vote was that social tensions were rising rapidly as the great depression set in. Bulgaria's ability to cope with this had been impaired by a decision in 1928 to return the country to the gold standard. The lev was over-valued and this forced the government to cut back on public expenditure. It also made it more difficult for Bulgaria to export her products. Bulgaria may not have suffered as much as some other nations because many of its peasants were prepared to accept the low standards of living which their retreat towards self-sufficiency dictated, but the suffering was still intense; between 1929 and 1933 peasant income per capita fell by a half. Many families were left with insufficient income to service their debts to the banks, to pay their taxes or to purchase those necessities they could not grow themselves. Workers in the towns who had little chance to grow any food of their own were even worse off and tension both in the towns and the countryside rose markedly.

The Bulgarian governments did what little was in their power to soften the effects of the great depression. Whilst still in office Lyapchev's administration established *Hranoiznos*, a state grain-purchasing agency which was also to be responsible for selling the grain on the international market. There was little *Hranoiznos* could do to increase world prices, but at least it provided the peasant producer with a guaranteed purchaser, and in later years, as prices recovered, the organisation increased in influence and was given responsibility for other crops such as tobacco. *Hranoiznos* in the 1930s owed much to Stamboliĭski's thwarted grain consortium of the previous decade.

The People's Bloc was also influenced by agrarian precedent. In September 1931 a law was introduced regulating the industrial and commercial cartels which had grown up in Bulgaria since the beginning of the 20th century. With some justification they had been an object of suspicion by the peasantry. Following the September law a government commission was established to regulate the prices of a number of essential products, including soap, sugar, cement, cotton goods, and gas. Steps were also taken to lighten tax burdens and to make it easier for peasants to repay debts, some debts being reduced and many repayment periods extended. Such legislation was not confined to administrations which included agrarians, but many of the ideas behind the new laws had been fashioned and honed in discussions within agrarian circles.

The agrarians had benefited from the resurgence of radicalism brought about by the depression. But they were not the only beneficiaries. In the cities the BWP rapidly increased in strength and took a leading part in organising strikes and other demonstrations against rising social distress. The government responded by banning various BWP organisations but this did not prevent the party registering notable gains in local elections in November 1931. In February 1932 the BWP secured an absolute majority on Sofia city council. This was too much for the government which dissolved the council; not even the Turks would have dared take such a drastic measure. The government also expelled 15 of the BWP's 29 deputies from the parliament.

Radical resurgence was not a phenomenon confined to the left. As was to be expected in the context of the early 1930s right-wing populist movements became more active and influential. A number of fascist or semi-fascist groups appeared in the 1920s but in the early 1930s the most prominent was the National Social Movement (NSM) established by Tsankov in 1930. The NSM had many of the trappings of the fascist and Nazi movements with their parades, flags, uniforms and general political aggression. Tsankov decried class conflict and called for 'social nationalism' in which, he said, bolshevism and fascism would one day combine; meanwhile, Bulgaria had its own national characteristics and historic traditions and it must not import political systems from outside. But though by no means a *quantité négligeable* the NSM attracted more attention than support. In Bulgaria the right-wing nationalist grievances which fed fascism in Hungary and other countries already had a vehicle for its expression in the Macedonian organisations. In Bulgaria the communists were much stronger in the towns than they were elsewhere in Eastern Europe and in the countryside the peasant was not going to be weaned from his allegiance to the agrarians by the posturings of a professor. The theatricality of fascism was also alien to the reserved, retiring character of most Bulgarians, especially the peasantry.

Not all radical responses to Bulgaria's problems in the late 1920s and early 1930s were populist. In 1927, Dimo Kazasov, a prominent Social Democrat before the party expelled him for serving as a minister under Tsankov, established a new journal, *Zveno* (Link). It was an influential publication and from it grew a political grouping which borrowed the journal's name. Zveno insisted that it was not a political party but it had a programme for national rebirth. This was based upon a rejection of the existing political parties whose corruption and constant squabbling, it said, had incapacitated the machinery of government. The *zvenari* also demanded a foreign policy based upon closer ties with the western European powers, something which could best be achieved through improving relations with Yugoslavia. Within Bulgaria the *zvenari* wanted a cleansing of political structures. They were not democrats; they were elitist, etatist and authoritarian. Their support was to be found mainly in the intelligentsia and in the more republican sections of the army, including the Military League.

At the end of 1933 Zveno decided that the country could no longer endure the existing system. The People's Bloc which had enjoyed considerable public support when it came to office had, not surprisingly, proved incapable of saving the country from the depression. What was worse was that it degenerated into the bad old habits of Bulgarian politics and in 1933 there was a public and very unseemly squabble between the Bloc's constituent parties over the re-allocation of cabinet posts. Gichev's agrarians were as culpable as the other groups.

This squabbling over the spoils of office was only one of a number of last straws as far as Zveno was concerned. Another was the fear that the king might purge the officer corps, removing its republican and its anti-Macedonian elements. Another was the rising power of the NSM. This was underlined in February 1934 when Tsankov's movement performed surprisingly well in local elections after which it became known that in May Hermann Göring would pay a private visit to Bulgaria, a visit which would coincide with a large NSM rally planned for 21 May.

The rally did not take place. On 19 May 1934 Zveno executed a swift, bloodless and entirely successful coup. It had been planned by Colonel Damyan Velchev, who had republican leanings, but it was a civilian member of Zveno, Kimon

Georgiev, who became head of the new government. Parliamentary democracy in Bulgaria, always a tender plant, had once more been trampled underfoot. It was not to flower again until the 1990s.

11
Through Authoritarianism towards Totalitarianism (1934–44)

Once in office Georgiev moved immediately to implement Zveno's programme which could be summarized as 'centralisation, rationalisation and modernisation'. In the political sense centralisation meant the concentration of power in the hands of the new government. To this end the political parties were disbanded and the national assembly dissolved, its competences being passed to the executive. Local democracy was also curtailed, with more power being given to the centre. Bulgaria's 16 regions were abolished and in their place there were to be seven provinces whose chief executive would not be elected but nominated by the government in Sofia. The elected mayors who had been a feature of Bulgarian political life since the liberation of 1878 were also to disappear, replaced by centrally appointed figures, all of whom were to be educated at least to secondary level and to have some legal training. The newly appointed officials were usually career civil servants with an eye to furthering their own careers and had few links to the local community; they became known as 'Flying Dutchmen'. That many of them had been active officials during the Tsankovist terror naturally added to their unpopularity.

The government of 19 May wanted to replace the former representative democracy of parliament and local councils with new concepts which synthesised agrarian and fascist ideas. A new assembly was to be created in which only a quarter of the members would represent 'the political element'; the others would represent the 'estates' which made up society. These, by the *zvenari*'s definition were workers, peasants, craftsmen, merchants, intelligentsia, civil servants and the free professions. Local councils were to be refashioned on similar lines, with only half the members being elected and then to represent the estates not geographic constituencies; the other half were to be nominated by senior officials. These notions were also used to break up the existing trade unions which were held to represent class rather than estate interests. From 1935 there was only one permitted trade union, the Bulgarian Workers' Union, which was organised on an estate basis. Membership was voluntary but the Union attracted many recruits.

Zveno abided by its determination not to be or be seen as a political party. It did, however, attempt to exercise influence over every aspect of national life. Its chief vehicle for doing this was the Directorate for Social Renewal (DSR). Predictably this was a centralised, hierarchical organisation whose purpose was 'to direct the cultural and intellectual life of the country towards unity and renewal'. To this end it monitored and attempted to control the press, the radio and the arts. The DSR also sought to preach the new government's programme through a series of public meetings and lectures. Like most similar organisations of its day the DSR paid particular attention to the nation's youth, but neither the public lectures or the courting of the nation's young met with conspicuous success.

Where the government of 19 May did achieve success was in foreign policy. Bulgaria's russophile traditions were strong and Zveno's opening of diplomatic relations with the Soviet Union in July 1934 was widely welcomed in Bulgaria. More important in the first half of the 1930s was the implementation of the Zveno's plans for better relations with Yugoslavia. Here the atmosphere had been gradually improving since the Pirot agreements and in October 1933 King Alexander of Yugoslavia had paid an official visit to Bulgaria. When he did so 10,000 Macedonians were moved out of Sofia to remote villages in the countryside. The Macedonian question, despite the gradual thaw in relations between Belgrade and Sofia since the Pirot agreements, was still central to Bulgarian-Yugoslav relations, the more so after the London convention of 1933 had included in its definition of an aggressor states any which supported or failed to take effective measures against armed units which operated from its territory. Then in 1934 came the Balkan entente between Yugoslavia, Romania, Greece and Turkey. This proved to have little bite but it worried the Bulgarian government because it was a recreation of the disastrous anti-Bulgarian alliance of 1913. Facing these dangers the Zveno government sent the army into the Petrich enclave and dispersed the IMRO activists. The move was sudden, bold, popular, unexpected and entirely successful. It transformed relations between Bulgaria and Yugoslavia and made possible the serious efforts at a rapprochement which were soon to be undertaken.

They were not to be taken by the *zvenari*. There were divisions between those who believed that now political power had been taken a mass movement should be created to preserve that power, and those who clung to the former belief that Zveno should not become a political party. The movement did not have widespread popular backing, its support coming mainly from the narrow ranks of senior professional administrators and the officer corps. And the latter could not be entirely relied upon. Velchev and his closest associates were generally believed to have republican sympathies but if it came to a contest between them and the monarchy most officers would probably remain loyal to their oath of allegiance to the king. Zveno therefore depended on the king remaining neutral and outside the political arena. In January 1935 it became known that he was no longer prepared to do this. In that month Georgiev and Velchev were removed from power with even greater ease than they had seized it less than a year before.

The second half of the 1930s was dominated by a search for a new constitution and by the adjustments in foreign policy made necessary by events in the centre of Europe. The king's first task was to try and clip the army's political wings. Velchev had gone into exile after the end of the Zveno government but he was tricked into returning and promptly arrested, tried and in February 1936 sentenced to death. The king commuted the sentence but he used the Velchev trial as a pretext to dissolve the Military League and to sack a number of known republicans in the officer corps.

Boris wanted to find a middle road between the extremes of left and right, both of which seemed to be gaining in strength. Tsankov and his NSM were encouraged by the successes of Hitler and Mussolini whilst the communists received a boost when their leader, Georgi Dimitrov, made a fool of Göring during the Reichstag fire trial in Leipzig in 1933.

They were also cashing in on rising industrial unrest and

took a hand in organising a number of strikes, including one by the tobacco workers in Plovdiv in 1936. Boris said he wanted a 'tidy and disciplined' democracy but that was little more than a euphemism for tighter central control. When elections were eventually held in March 1938 the franchise was restricted and the voting spread over three days in case the police had to be moved from one place to another; married women and widows were allowed to vote for the first time but for them voting was not compulsory as it was for men. The newly elected assembly was smaller than previous ones but it also proved less amenable than hoped and was therefore dissolved. The general election of December 1939 was even more controlled than the previous one.

Born in the Radomir district in 1882 to a Protestant family, Georgi Dimitrov became a member of the socialist party in 1902. He aligned with the Narrow socialists and was elected to its central committee in 1909. He was a leader of the general strike of 1919–20 and of the communist uprising in 1923 after which he went into exile. He had for some years been prominent in the Comintern. After the Leipzig trial he was given Soviet citizenship and went to Moscow where he became head of the Comintern. When he was made prime minister of Bulgaria in November 1946 he was already ill and died in July 1949.

By the end of the 1930s foreign affairs inevitably preoccupied Boris and his ministers. Their prime objective was to remain neutral. The desire to preserve good relations with Britain and France had meant a cooling of those with Italy whose actions in Abyssinia and the Spanish Civil War had angered London and Paris. Nor would too close association with Hitler's Germany be acceptable to the British and French, besides which it might over-excite Tsankov and his followers. On the other hand the resurgent Germany could not be offended. The safest course seemed to be to seek regional security through improved relations with the other Balkan states, above all

Yugoslavia. The suppression of the Petrich Macedonians had made this easier but it was not until January 1937 that a treaty of friendship between Bulgaria and Yugoslavia was signed. In the following year in the Salonica agreements all the Balkan states renounced war and, to prove their good intent, also sanctioned all round rearmament.

But there was an unconquerable dilemma facing Bulgaria. It wished to remain neutral and avoid war, but it was also a revisionist state and popular opinion wanted some redefinition of Neuilly. As Mussolini and even more so Hitler went from success to success, revisionism became not only desirable but possible. After the Vienna agreements of November 1938 Bulgaria was the only defeated state which had not received some territorial redress. Public opinion could not be unaware of this. It made the extreme right more attractive. And it was one of the factors which increased German influence.

Another pull towards Germany was commerce. The 'blocked marks' system introduced in 1932 and extended by the Nazis provided a clever short-term means for helping economic recovery. The Germans agreed to buy primary produce from states such as Bulgaria but the money was not paid to those states directly but deposited in closed accounts in Berlin; the funds in these accounts could only be used to purchase German manufactured goods. Amongst German exports, of course, were armaments. Stamboliĭski's government had been more than content to abide by the military restrictions imposed by Neuilly but it had not been able to prevent some evasion of them, with soldiers hiding munitions and weapons in secret dumps, for example. By the middle of the 1930s, with Germany having renounced any limitations on its armed forces, Bulgaria began to rearm, purchasing its weapons mainly, though not entirely, from Germany.

A number of Bulgarian officers were also sent to train in Germany, one of the few states willing to provide this facility. As Boris well knew, rearmament would give soldiers things to do and take their minds off politics.

Increasing German economic influence did not in itself push Bulgaria into the German camp. The Nazi-Soviet pact made it possible for Bulgaria to be well disposed both its traditional friend and to its best prospect for contemporary territorial gain. Boris still would not commit himself, once remarking, 'My army is pro-German, my wife is Italian, my people are pro-Russian, I alone am pro-Bulgarian.'[1] In 1940, however, he did replace his incumbent prime minister with the strongly pro-German Bogdan Filov. Some anti-Semitic legislation was then enacted, as was a defence of the realm act granting the government wide powers of arrest. German victories and the entry of Italy into the war in early summer forced some recalculations in Sofia where it was believed that the British navy would now be excluded from the eastern Mediterranean. The German conquest of France also precipitated the Soviet acquisition of Bessarabia and the Bukovina from Romania. In September an enfeebled Romania was forced by Hitler and Stalin to cede the southern Dobrudja to Bulgaria. Even this could not persuade Boris to shift from neutrality and he rejected both an offer from Mussolini which would have given Bulgaria western Thrace if it joined Italy's forthcoming attack on Greece, and a secret proposal by Stalin under which Bulgaria would become part of a Soviet 'security zone'. By the end of 1940 Hitler had decided to attack the Soviet Union and to intervene in the Balkans to aid Mussolini's flagging campaign in Albania and Greece. German troops massing in Romania in preparation for the intended assault on the Soviet Union would be moved to Greece and the easiest path would be via Bulgaria. German troops would pass through Bulgaria whatever the Bulgarians might feel and it was therefore better, said a senior army officer, that they did so 'as friends rather than as enemies'.[2] On 1 March 1941 Filov signed the tripartite pact. Bulgaria's joining the Axis was endorsed by the sŭbranie despite intense protest from the few opposition deputies still left in it. When Hitler decided to attack Yugoslavia in April 1941 in order to remove an anti-Nazi government in Belgrade Bulgaria participated in the action. Bulgaria's immediate award was to be given back the lost western territories and to have administrative rights in Macedonia and western Thrace, with full ownership to be conferred at the end of the war.

The British legation had left Sofia in March but a formal state of war did not exist until December 1941 when, after the Japanese attack on Pearl Harbor, Bulgaria declared war on both Britain and the United States. Bulgaria did not declare war on the Soviet Union, Boris and his ministers insisting that russophilia was so deeply embedded in the Bulgarian national psyche that the peasant conscripts would not be dependable if pitted against the Russians. Furthermore, it was argued, the Bulgarian army was not sufficiently well equipped to fight a modern, armoured campaign such as that on the Eastern Front. Bulgaria's main contribution to the Axis war effort was to provide troops for occupation duties in Serbia, thus releasing German units to fight against the Red Army.

The Bulgarian decision not to participate in the war against the Soviet Union was a cause of some friction between Sofia and Berlin. So too was Bulgarian policy with regard to the Jews. There had been protests in 1940 at the anti-Semitic legislation introduced in that year but there was outrage when it was learned that arrangements had been made to deport 6,000 of Bulgaria's 50,000 Jews to Poland. In typical Balkan fashion the secret had become public because it was leaked to the press by the mistress of one of those involved in drawing up the plans. The protest began with deputies from Kyustendil, the town in which the Jews were to be concentrated before deportation, but it rapidly spread through virtually all sections of Bulgarian society; illiterate peasants signed petitions with their thumbprints, workers from all trades staged demonstrations, the Bishop of Plovdiv said he would lie down in front of any train removing Jews, and even Tsankov voiced his disapproval. When presented with a petition signed by 43 pro-government members of the national assembly the king immediately overruled the decision to deport the Jews. In May the Nazis and their Bulgarian acolytes made another attempt to deport Bulgarian Jews but once again they faced insuperable public hostility, led this time by the head of the Bulgarian Orthodox Church. The Jews of Bulgaria were saved, but they had to spend the remainder of the war in grim circumstances, wearing the yellow star, living in detention camps and working on public projects.

The argument used with the Germans had been that Bulgaria's Jews were Bulgarian subjects whose fate could be decided only by the Bulgarian authorities. In the end the Germans accepted this. The Jews in Bulgaria's newly-acquired territories were less fortunate. In August 1942 the sŭbranie had voted that they should be denied Bulgarian citizenship. In March 1943 they were deported to the camps in Poland where all but a tiny fraction perished.

The expansion of Bulgaria into Thrace and Macedonia had originally been popular with Bulgarians. Most of San Stefano Bulgaria had been regained; the Church was united with its lost provinces; and Boris was greeted as the 'King Unifier'. The newly acquired territories received some benefits too; over 800 new schools were built and the King Boris University, established in Skopje, was Macedonia's first institute of higher learning.

In August 1943 the situation altered drastically with the sudden death of King Boris. He was succeeded by his son, Simeon II. Because Simeon was a minor a three-man regency was formed in which the dominant figure was Filov. Boris's death unsettled the nation just as the war was beginning to turn against the Germans who had been driven out of North Africa, were losing the battle of the Atlantic and, most dramatically, had lost the initiative on the Eastern Front with the failure to take Stalingrad. Boris had insisted that Bulgaria would wage only 'symbolic war' against Britain and the United States, but the Allies had other ideas. At the end of 1943 and early in 1944 the war became anything but symbolic as the RAF and the USAAF pounded Sofia with high explosives and incendiaries; for ten days in January the country was virtually without any administration because so many civil servants had fled the devastated capital.

King Boris's death on 28 August 1943 at the age of 48 occasioned great speculation. He had recently returned from a visit to Hitler. The men spoke without interpreters so no record of their conversations exists but it was thought there had been disagreements over Bulgaria's commitment to the war. On the journey back to Bulgaria Boris's plane was forced to fly at high altitude and oxygen masks became necessary. Some believe Boris was poisoned by German agents. There seems little reason to reject the official explanation that he died of a brain haemorrhage, perhaps occasioned by his climbing Bulgaria's highest mountain soon after his return.

Filov turned to the Soviets, hoping that they might intercede and persuade the Allies to end the air attacks, but the response was not encouraging and by the spring Moscow was making its own demands, not least that German troops leave Bulgaria and that Bulgaria cease allowing German warships to use Bulgarian ports. Filov was forced to turn to the Allies. Peace feelers had been put out in the summer of 1943 but the Allies had laid down harsh conditions if any deal were to be struck. They were no more willing to compromise in the early months of 1944. But by now Filov was facing a further difficulty: armed resistance at home.

Resistance movements had not been strong in Bulgaria which was not a defeated or an occupied country. The Pladne agrarians, however, had opposed Bulgarian participation in the war from the very beginning. Their leader, Georgi M Dimitrov, known as 'Gemeto' ('the G M') to distinguish him from the communist leader with same name and initials, worked closely with the British who smuggled him out of Bulgaria when his party's activities were uncovered by the police in the spring of 1941. After the Nazi invasion of the Soviet Union in June 1941 the Bulgarian communists joined the opposition and began to organise resistance activity. The political arm of the resistance was the Fatherland Front (FF). The first FF had been formed in 1941 by a number of leftist factions with the communists, acting on orders from Moscow, leading the way. It was the communists' determination to dominate the organisation which brought about its collapse. It was reformed in February 1942 with four constituent groups: the communists, Zveno, a Social Democratic faction, and the Pladne agrarians. The FF insisted that it was not a party but 'a mass organisation of all the people which on the basis of its programme unites the widest spectrum of the popular masses irrespective of their political allegiance'.[3]

In June 1944 Filov replaced his prime minister with one more likely, it was hoped, to placate the Allies. It was a false hope. Bulgaria was subjected to mounting pressures: the Soviets were demanding real action to remove the Germans, something which Filov rejected because, he said, it would precipitate a full-scale German takeover as had happened in Hungary in March; the western Allies were proving ever more unaccommodating when it came to peace talks; there were alarming signs that Turkey was about to declare war; and there was the partisan movement which, though never more than an irritant, was a factor which had to be considered.

In the final event it was the Red Army which decided the issue. In early August it achieved a major breakthrough in Romania and by the end of the month it was on the banks of the Danube. There followed ten days of chaos which produced another change of government, the new prime minister being Konstantin Muraviev, an agrarian and a nephew of Stamboliïski. He attempted to placate the Russians by declaring war on Germany but it did not work and the Russians declared war on him; for a few days Bulgaria was at war with all the major powers involved in the Second World War except Japan. A Bulgarian involved in those climacteric events lamented, 'history had allowed only three days for the solution of questions which could not be decided in the previous three years'.[4] On 8 September, with the FF staging strikes and protests throughout the country, the Red Army crossed the Danube and entered Bulgaria.

On 9 September 1944 military units in Sofia staged a coup against a government which had in reality ceased to exist. A new administration was formed by the FF.

12

Stamboliĭski's Legacy

Immediately after the end of the First World War Bulgarian politics had been dominated by a contest between the radical agrarians and the communists to fill the vacuum left by collapse of a discredited system. From that contest the agrarians emerged victorious. After the Second World War precisely the same contest was seen, but with precisely the opposite result.

∞∞∞∞

Agrarianism had taken deep roots in Bulgaria. In 1923 its political manifestation, the BANU, had been brutally removed from power, but much of the Stamboliĭski regime's legislation remained in force. The land redistribution scheme was not stopped, though the amount of land allowed to individual families was increased; the CLS remained, though all women, not just Muslims, were now to be exempt from it; the building of cooperative blocs of flats continued throughout the inter-war years and into communist times, whilst social legislation such as the eight-hour day, the progressive income tax and the refugee relief act also remained on the statute book.

Royal rule had meant the end of party political activity but the rudiments of the BANU's apparatus survived under other names and agrarianism did not lose its appeal for the peasant masses. That appeal increased during the Second World War.

When the FF took power in September 1944 the communists who dominated it faced a number of problems when trying to weaken the agrarians' standing in the country. Unlike in Poland, Czechoslovakia, Hungary or eastern Germany there were no large estates which they could divide up and parcel out to peasants who would then, it was presumed, owe them a debt of gratitude. There was also no doubt that in Bulgaria the agrarians, however divided they had been, were the most popular political force and their membership grew much more rapidly than that of the communists. The latter soon disposed of Gemeto on grounds of his being in British pay and he fled in April 1945 to escape arrest. This in fact did more to strengthen than weaken the agrarians because Nikola Petkov then took over. He had lost a father and a brother to political assassins and had an enviable record of opposition to the recent war and of resistance activity in it; he was by far the most popular politician in the country. The communist response was to engineer yet another split in the now apparently reunited BANU. The ministry of justice, which was under communist domination, declared that the pro-communist faction under Aleksandŭr Obbov was the rightful owner of the BANU's newspaper and property. Petkov immediately set up a new party, the Bulgarian Agrarian National Union-Nikola Petkov (BANU-NP).

In the summer of 1945 it secured a notable victory. The

end of the war in Europe had made elections possible but the communists were insisting, with Soviet support, that all the FF parties appear on a single list and that in the distribution of seats the agrarians and the communists would have the same number, 95. Petkov maintained that an accurate measure of the relative popularity of the two parties would give the agrarians three times as many deputies as the communists, and he demanded that the elections be postponed until the issue had been settled. In this he had the backing of the British and American representatives on the Allied Control Commission (ACC), the body which was to supervise the affairs of Bulgaria until full sovereignty was restored with the signing of a peace treaty. The elections were postponed until November. His victory greatly increased Petkov's popularity and within two months over two thousand new BANU-NP *druzhbi* were founded. But Petkov did not succeed in his demand that the single list system be abolished and in pique he ordered his supporters to boycott the poll.

At the end of 1945 western diplomatic pressure procured another advance for the agrarians; the Soviets agreed that the coalition government in Bulgaria should be widened but Petkov overplayed his hand, demanding that as the most popular party the BANU-NP be given the post of prime minister and that the communists give up control of the ministries of justice and of the interior. With Soviet backing, they refused. For the next year and a half the communists chipped away at the BANU-NP and the other opposition parties, limiting their press by restricting supplies of newsprint, disrupting their meetings, threatening their members with violence and denying them official jobs. These methods inevitably had some effect but not as much as the communists had hoped. The next major test of national opinion was the general election of October 1946 for a Grand National Assembly. The communists secured more votes than anyone else. They had 53 per cent but the opposition had 28 per cent and the non-communist FF parties 17 per cent, and this in the face of considerable intimidation and interference by the communists at the polling stations. More indicative of the opinions of the general populace rather of the political activists was the ratio of party membership to votes gained; for every BWP (Communist) party member there were 5.4 votes from members of the public but for every BANU-NP member there were 15. And the three regions in which the communists failed to secure a majority of the votes were Varna, Pleven and Rusé, all in the north-east of Bulgaria where agrarianism had been born.[1]

But the political situation in Bulgaria was now to be changed not by internal national factors but by developments on the international stage. In February 1947 a peace treaty between Bulgaria and the Allies was signed in Paris. Under its provisions the Red Army, which had been in Bulgaria since September 1944, was to leave nine months after ratification of the treaty. The communists had always believed that the Red Army was the ultimate weapon it could wield to enforce its will. Petkov believed this too, and drew the conclusion that when the Red Army left the communists would be greatly weakened. He took further encouragement from the promulgation of the Truman Doctrine in March and therefore went on the offensive, ridiculing the communists' resistance record and showing that they were spending far more on police than had the authoritarian regimes of 1934–44. Dimitrov hit back. He too believed that the departure of the Soviet forces would weaken him so he acted whilst it was still on hand to help if necessary. On 5 June Petkov was arrested in the sŭbranie, an illegal act, and then subjected to a horrendous show trial in which he was denied a defence lawyer. Many of the prosecution witnesses had clearly been tortured but their evidence was enough to secure a conviction. Petkov was hanged and, though one of the few leading Bulgarian politicians with genuine religious convictions, was denied the last rites and a Christian burial.

The arrest of Petkov destroyed the old agrarian party and in August the BANU-NP was dissolved and its property confiscated. Those deputies who had remained loyal to Petkov were either removed from the GNA or were told that in future opposition to the government would not be tolerated. Asen Stamboliĭski, son of the great leader, was one of those deputies. After the liquidation of the independent agrarian party came the destruction of its social basis through the process of collectivisation. Begun soon after 1945 with financial pressures the campaign ended with compulsion to which peasants in many areas offered resolute but ineffective resistance.

Agrarianism had taken such strong root amongst the Bulgarian nation, however, that it could not be entirely eliminated. In the period immediately after the Second World War the communists were not prepared to enter coalitions without it and thus they set up the subservient Obbov group which bore the name of Stamboliĭski's party. But even after total communist supremacy had been achieved the BANU lived on. It was a peculiar feature of communist rule in Bulgaria that there were two large, theoretically independent parties, the BCP and the BANU. In the early 1960s the ruler of communist Bulgaria, Todor Zhivkov, sought to strengthen his power base in the countryside. He did so by making the BANU leader, Georgi Traĭkov, head of state. It also became common practice for the head of the BANU to attend BCP politburo meetings when agricultural questions were under discussion, though the major decisions were always taken by the communist hierarchs. If the BANU had little real political power it had considerable social influence. It was wealthy and many in the countryside still turned to it rather than the BCP for advice, social contact or even loans.

The BANU also had members in all Bulgarian cabinets during communist rule. Ironically, the first purely communist administration in the country was formed in 1990, after the foundations of communist power had been undermined. By then the BANU wanted to shake itself free of its embarrassing ties with the communists, not least because the BANU-NP had re-emerged to solicit for the agrarian vote. But by this time agrarianism was a spent force. Collectivisation had done away with the historic peasant proprietor which it had been the BANU's function to protect and promote.

Born in Pravets in 1911 Todor Zhivkov moved to Sofia as a teenager and became a printer and a trade union activist. His wartime activities are obscure but after 1944 he gained influence through his job of distributing confiscated wealth to party bigwigs. He became party boss in 1954 and was to become the longest serving communist party boss in Europe, remaining in office until November 1989. He survived an attempted military coup in 1965 and thereafter neutralised threats by moving potential rivals from one post to another. He relied heavily on Soviet backing. When Gorbachev came to power in 1985 this ceased because Zhivkov represented the old, gerontocracy which Gorbachev wished to see replaced. Zhivkov died in 1998.

ooooo

But if agrarianism was no longer a major contestant in the political arena, the historic legacy of Stamboliĭski remained and it was one which few other agrarian leaders could equal. Poland's Wincenty Witos had been restricted, as were all

Polish politicians of his day, by the need constantly to construct and maintain coalitions, and his power had been greatest in his native Galician region. Antonín Švehla also had to operate within the restrictions of a coalition though through the odd, extra-constitutional mechanisms which evolved in inter-war Czechoslovakia he had become a central figure in national politics. But his programme was much less radical than Stamboliĭski's. In Romania the able Iuliu Maniu had enjoyed office only for a short period, and it was a period dominated by the unwelcome return of a departed monarch and the onset of the great depression; he had not had enough time to implement his programme which, like Švehla's, was less adventurous than Stamboliĭski's. Time had been short, too, for Albania's nearest equivalent to an agrarian reformer, Bishop Fan Noli. Outside Bulgaria the most powerful agrarian party had been that led by Stjepan Radić in Croatia. His policies, however, had been inextricably interwoven with the Croats' desire to secure greater devolution in the new Yugoslavia, besides which Radić's sometimes unpredictable behaviour had limited his party's effectiveness.

No agrarian leader in Europe had had the complete domination over the national parliament which Stamboliĭski enjoyed, and no other had carried out so wide-ranging a reform programme. Stamboliĭski was also the only agrarian leader to have been head of government in a vanquished state. Perhaps if he had been prime minister of a victorious country European agrarianism would have fared better and the fate of the Green International would have been different.

As it was agrarianism, so powerful in the confused world of the early 1920s, declined in significance. It faced competition from other new creeds. In some countries, Romania for example, its populism led it close to the rising force of fascism whilst, as has been noted, the powerful Croatian party become hoisted by its own, nationalist, petard. By the second half of the 1930s Europe was swinging rapidly away from the cooperative notions which underlay not only agrarianism's internal policies, but its attitudes towards foreign policy. There was little point in preaching international peasant fraternity, and the rejection of nationalism and territorial aspirations when aggressive fascist and Nazi policies were destabilising the continent.

Soviet-style communism was a further threat to agrarianism. Initially it was a rival radical movement but after Stalin's adoption of forced collectivisation it was, in ideological terms, a deadly enemy. In the 1930s Soviet-style forced economic reconstruction, and socialism, captured the intellectual high-ground of opposition to the extreme right and by the end of the Second World War planned, industrialised economies with agriculture and the peasantry playing a subordinate role to industry and the proletariat had become the norm in Europe outside the semi-fascist relics of Iberia.

In the late 1960s and early 1970s agrarianism attracted the attention of scholars, particularly in the United States, and some of the best works on the subjects were written then.[2] It was not just that agrarianism had been neglected but it chimed with the growing feeling that industrialisation and urbanisation had brought problems as well as benefits. Socialism just as much as capitalism encouraged these processes. Agrarian ideas were not entirely removed from the then fashionable notion of 'Small is Beautiful'. The Soviet suppression of the reforming Dubček regime in Czechoslovakia in 1968 was a further incentive to find an alternative to the existing ideologies dominating the world.

In Bulgaria after the fall of the totalitarian system in

1989–90 the BANU-NP was reconstituted but it made relatively little impact. The world had passed it by. Collectivisation had destroyed the small peasant proprietor upon which
agrarianism had been based and in a world dominated by
rampant market forces notions of cooperation carried little
weight. But the legacy of its greatest Bulgarian theorist and
practitioner remains respected in his native land. A major
boulevard in Sofia still bears his name and his statue, like
those of Vasil Levski and Tsar Alexander II of Russia (the
Tsar Liberator), but unlike that of Lenin, remains.

If Stamboliĭski's name and image are still revered in contemporary Bulgaria the treaty he signed single-handedly at
Neuilly and the war which had proceeded it are given little
commemoration. No nation wishes to recall defeat and
humiliation. What does survive in some quarters is a feeling
of resentment at the treaty's terms. When, in a broadcast on
the BBC Bulgarian Service I ventured the opinion that, com-
pared to Austria, Hungary or Germany, Bulgaria had not been
treated harshly by the peacemakers of 1919 I took a considerable amount of flak from a number of Bulgarians. For many
the loss of Macedonia was an injustice and a flagrant viola-
tion of the notion of national self-determination. A further
resentment was the non-fulfilment of Article 48. This inflicted
considerable damage on Bulgaria's economic development
and it weakened the moral position of the treaty powers.
Their insistence that Bulgaria obey the terms of the treaty
had to be heeded but Bulgarians could legitimately ask why
those powers remained deaf to pleas that Bulgaria be given
the economic outlet to the Aegean it had been promised.

The First World War was a huge factor in determining the
future of all states. Bulgaria was no exception. Its national
ambitions had been thwarted, an experience made all the

more bitter because it was the second time in half a decade that Bulgaria had been forced to relinquish much of its prized territorial aspirations. For most Bulgarians the aspirations remained. They were, perforce, suppressed immediately after 1919 but when Europe was again reconstructed during the Second World War they resurfaced. It was not, perhaps, until Bulgaria joined the European Union in January 2007 that territorial expansion was given up as a national aspiration. The European Union is far from the agrarian confederation of which Stamboliĭski dreamed but it is a move away from the nation state towards a pooling of sovereignty; it is, to borrow the phrase he used when writing to the head of the Romanian delegation in Neuilly, *a political organisation coming together at a higher level*. Bulgaria's evolution since the First World War has been long, complicated and tortuous but in this at least one of the benefits for which Stamboliĭski hoped has been achieved.

Notes

1 The Emergence of Modern Bulgaria

1. It is brilliantly analysed in Paul Stephenson, *The Legend of Basil the Bulgar Slayer* (Cambridge: 2003).

2 Bulgarian Society and the Birth of the BANU

1. Aleksandŭr Stamboliĭski, *Izbrani proizvedeniya* (Sofia: 1979) p 41, hereafter Stamboliĭski, *Izb proiz.*

3 The Rise of Aleksandŭr Stamboliĭski

1. Misha Glenny, *The Balkans* (London: 1999) p 336.
2. A L Kennedy, 'A Peasant Statesman', *Fortnightly Review*, 114: 680 (1923) p 185, hereafter Kennedy.
3. H Charles Woods, 'The Internal Situation In Bulgaria', *Fortnightly Review*, 109: 654 (1921) p 1040.
4. Mari Firkatian, *Diplomats and Dreamers* (Lanham MD: 2008) p 202, hereafter Firkatian.
5. Nikola D Petkov, *Aleksandŭr Stamboliĭski; lichnost i idei po dokumenti sŭbrani i podredeni ot Nikola D Petkov* (Varna: 1991) p 68, hereafter Petkov, *Lichnost.*

6. Aleksandŭr Stamboliĭski, *Politicheski Partii ili sŭslovni organisatsiya?* (Sofia: 1909) p 62, hereafter Stamboliĭski, *Politicheski Partii.*

7. Petkov, *Lichnost*, p 65.

8. Stamboliĭski, *Izb proiz*, p 87.

9. These were the headings he used in an article written in prison and entitled, 'The Difference Between the Agrarian Union and the Parties'. The article is reprinted in Petkov, *Lichnost*, pp 123–8.

10. Petkov, *Lichnost*, p 170. Stamboliĭski was speaking to the Grand National Assembly (parliament) in 1911.

11. Stamboliĭski, *Izb proiz*, p 108.

4 The Years of War (1912–18)

1. Cited in John D Bell, *Peasants in Power: Aleksandŭr Stamboliski and the Bulgarian Agrarian National Union, 1983–1923* (Princeton NJ: 1977) p 92, hereafter Bell.

2. Stamboliĭski, *Politicheski Partii*, pp 90–1.

3. John Julius Norwich (ed), *The Duff Cooper Diaries* (London: 2005) p 11.

4. The statue is opposite the sŭbranie building. For the speech see Petkov, *Lichnost*, p 8.

5. Winston S Churchill, *The World Crisis 1911–18* (London: 1960) p 317.

6. Stamboliĭski, *Izb proiz*, p 147.

7. Cited by Lyudomir Ognyanov, 'Antivoennata deĭnost na Aleksandŭr Stamboliĭski (1914–1918g)', *Istoricheski Pregled*, 35/2 (1979) p 26.

8. Cited in Raĭko Daskalov, *Politicheska i dŭrzhavna deĭnost. Privetstviya i dokladi, izneseni na natsionalnoto tŭrzhestveno sŭbranie i na nauchnata sesiya po sluchaĭ*

100 godini ot rozhdeneto na Raĭko Daskalov, no editor named (Sofia: 1988) p 77.

9. The record of the conversation so far cited is taken from Aleksandŭr Stamboliĭski, *Dvete mi sreshti s Tsar Ferdinand* (Sofia: 1919) pp 13–16.

10. This final quotation is taken from the version of the conversation given in Bell and is based on Stamboliĭski's *Dvete mi sreshti*. None of those present ever questioned the veracity of Stamboliĭski's account.

11. Stamboliĭski, *Izb proiz*, p 183.

5 Bulgaria's Exit from the War

1. David Lloyd George, *War Memoirs* (London: 1933–6) Vol. vi, pp 3119, 3215–17.

2. Charles Keserich and George D Herron, 'The United States and Peacemaking with Bulgaria, 1918–1919', *East European Quarterly*, 14:1 (1980) pp 39–44, hereafter Keserich and Herron.

3. Keserich and Herron, pp 45–6.

4. Cited in Bell, p 185.

5. See Nadezhda Muir, *Dmitri Stancioff; Patriot and Cosmopolitan, 1864–1940* (London: 1957) p 208, hereafter Muir.

6. Muir, p 208.

6 The Treaty of Neuilly

1. Muir, p 209.

2. H M V Temperley (ed), *A History of the Peace Conference of Paris*, (London: 1920–1924) Vol. iv, p 411, hereafter Temperley.

3. Firkatian, p 191.

4. Petkov, *Lichnost*, p 41.

5. Bell, pp 187–8.
6. Petkov, *Lichnost*, p 97.
7. Temperley, iv, p 168 n3.
8. Temperley, iv, p 457.
9. Temperley iv, p 458.
10. Petkov, *Lichnost*, p 98.
11. Kennedy, p 180.

7 Stamboliïski and the Restrictions of the Treaty of Neuilly

1. Firkatian, p 211.
2. E L Woodward and Rohan Butler (eds), *Documents on British Foreign Policy, 1919–1939*, series 1 (London: 1947–86) Vol. xii, p 481.
3. Firkatian, p 204.
4. Cited Bell, p 190.
5. E L Woodward and Rohan Butler (eds), *Documents on British Foreign Policy, 1919–1939*, series 1 (London: 1947–86) Vol. xii, p 490.
6. Firkatian, p 203.
7. Constantine Stephanove, 'Democratic Czar And Peasant Premier', *Current History* (New York), 14/6 (1921) p 997, hereafter Stephanove, 'Democratic Czar'.
8. Theodore Vladimiroff, 'Bulgaria's Novel Methods of Reconstruction', *Current History* (New York), 13/2 (1920) p 219, hereafter Vladimiroff.
9. Prof L E Textor, 'Belgrade and Sofia in the Spring of 1923', *Historical Outlook*, 15/2 (1924) p 68.
10. Stephanove, 'Democratic Czar', p 999.

8 Reparations and Foreign Policy

1. Lady Grogan, 'Bulgaria and the Treaty of Neuilly', *Contemporary Review*, 121 (1922) p 577, hereafter Grogan.
2. Grogan, p 578n.
3. Lt.-Col. The Honble. H D Napier, *The Experiences of a Military Attaché in the Balkans* (London: no date) p 265.
4. Kennedy, p 184.
5. Cited Bell, p 189.
6. Cited Bell, p 185.
7. Vladimiroff, p 220.
8. Stamboliĭski, *Izb proiz*, pp 259–60.
9. 'The Balkan States Growing Neighborly', *Current History* (New York), 14/4 (1921), p 699.
10. Cited in Constantine Stephanove, 'Bulgaria's Solution Of Post-War Problems', *Current History* (New York), 34/5 (1931) p 709, hereafter Stephanove, 'Bulgaria's Solution'.

9 The Fall of Stamboliĭski

1. Cited Firkatian, p 205.
2. Stephane Groueff, *Crown of Thorns* (Lanham, MD: 1987) p 100.
3. Konstantin Muraviev, *Sŭbitiya i hora: Spomeni*, ed. Ilcho Dimitrov (Sofia: 1992) p 67, hereafter Muraviev.
4. Stephanove, 'Bulgaria's Solution', p 709.
5. Muraviev, p 78.

10 From Coup to Coup (1923–34)

1. For a useful summary of the Rumbold commission, see Martin Gilbert, *Sir Horace Rumbold; Portrait of a Diplomat, 1869–1941* (London: 1973) pp 306–10.

11 Through Authoritarianism towards Totalitarianism (1934–44)

1. Marshall Lee Miller, *Bulgaria during the Second World War* (Stanford CA: 1975) p 1.
2. Cited in Dimitŭr Ĭonchev, *Bŭlgariya i Belomorieto (Oktomvri 1940–9 Septemvri 1944); Voennopoliticheski aspekti* (Sofia: 1993) p 25.
3. Quoted in Kiril Vasilev *et al* (eds), *Otechestven Front: Dokumenti i Materiali*, Vol. 1 part i (Sofia: 1987) p 360.
4. Valentin Aleksandrov, *Atanas Burov; banker, politik, diplomat* (Sofia: 1992) p 96.

12 Stamboliĭski's Legacy

1. See Vesselin T Dimitrov, *Stalin's Cold War: Soviet Foreign Policy, Democracy and Communism in Bulgaria, 1941–1948* (Basingstoke: 2008) p 159.
2. Above all that of John Bell. But see also, Frederick D Chary, 'Agrarians, Radicals, Socialists and the Bulgarian Peasantry, 1899–1905', in Ivan Volgyes (ed), *The Peasantry of Eastern Europe*, Vol. 1, *Roots of Rural Transformation* (Oxford: 1979) pp 35–56, and 'The Politicization of the Bulgarian Agrarian Popular Union, 1899–1901', in Dimitŭr Kosev (ed), *Bulgaria Past and Present*, (Sofia: 1982) pp 249–57; and Eric R Weissman, 'The Cooperative Movement in the Bulgarian Village prior to World War One' (Ph D thesis, University of Washington: 1977).

Chronology

YEAR	AGE	THE LIFE AND THE LAND
1878		Feb: Victorious Russian army dictates terms of peace to Ottomans at San Stefano; a huge new Bulgarian state is created.
		13 Jul: Treaty of Berlin truncates Bulgaria to small area between river Danube and Balkan mountains, and creates Eastern Rumelia, a province of the Ottoman Empire. Macedonia returned to Ottoman rule. Bulgaria is to be a vassal of the Ottoman sultan.
1879		1 Mar: Aleksandür Stamboliĭski (AS) born, in Slavovitsa in southern Bulgaria.
		Jul: Alexander Battenberg arrives as Prince of Bulgaria.
1885	6	6 Sep: Eastern Rumelia declares union with Bulgaria.
		Nov: Serbia attacks Bulgaria; Bulgarian victory at battle of Slivnitsa.
1886	7	Aug: Prince Alexander deposed by military coup, returns and then abdicates because of Russian disapproval.
1887	8	Jul: 'Foxy' Ferdinand of Saxe-Coburg-Gotha elected Prince of Bulgaria.
1893	14	AS wins place at place at the state agricultural school in Sadovo.

YEAR	HISTORY	CULTURE
1878	Assassination attempt on Kaiser Wilhelm I: Germany passes Anti-Socialist Law. Electric street lighting introduced in London.	Thomas Hardy, *The Return of the Native*. Algernon Charles Swinburne, *Poems and Ballads*.
1879	Zulu War. Alsace-Lorraine declared an integral part of Germany.	Henry James, *Daisy Miller*. Tchaikovsky, opera 'Eugen Onegin'.
1885	General Gordon killed in fall of Khartoum to the Mahdi. Germany annexes Tanganyika and Zanzibar.	Maupassant, *Bel Ami*. H Rider Haggard, *King Solomon's Mines*.
1886	Irish Home Rule Bill introduced by Prime Minister Gladstone. First Indian National Congress meets.	R L Stevenson, *Dr Jekyll and Mr Hyde*.
1887	Queen Victoria's Golden Jubilee. Failed coup by General Boulanger in Paris.	Arthur Conan Doyle, *A Study in Scarlet*. Van Gogh, painting 'Moulin de la Galette'.
1893	Franco-Russian alliance signed. Second Irish Home Rule Bill rejected by House of Lords.	Oscar Wilde, *A Woman of No Importance*. Art Nouveau appears in Europe.

YEAR	AGE	THE LIFE AND THE LAND
1895	16	AS moves to the state vinicultural institute in Pleven where he is a student until 1897.
1898	19	AS becomes a teacher in Vetren, a village near his birth place.
1899	20	Dec: AS attends founding congress of Agrarian Union in Pleven.
1900	21	May: AS publishes his first article in an agrarian newspaper.
		Summer: AS marries Milena Daskalova, a fellow teacher.
1901	22	AS studies philosophy in the University of Halle, Germany.
		Oct: Agrarian Union reorganised as the Bulgarian Agrarian National Union (BANU).
1902	23	Feb: AS returns to Bulgaria having contracted TB; is forced to abandon plans to study agronomy in Munich.
1903	24	AS becomes editorial assistant on *Zemedelsko zname* (Agrarian banner). He soon becomes editor.
		Aug: Large-scale uprising in Macedonia and Thrace is suppressed by Ottoman troops. Thousands flee to Bulgaria as refugees.
1905	26	AS plays leading part in working out programme of the BANU.

YEAR	HISTORY	CULTURE
1895	Sino-Japanese War ends. Armenians massacred in Ottoman Empire. Jameson Raid into Transvaal.	H G Wells, *The Time Machine*. Tchaikovsky, ballet 'Swan Lake'.
1898	Spanish-American War. Death of Bismarck.	Oscar Wilde, *The Ballad of Reading Gaol*.
1899	Outbreak of Second Boer War. First Peace Conference at the Hague.	Rudyard Kipling, *Stalky and Co*. Elgar, 'Enigma Variations'.
1900	Assassination of King Umberto I of Italy. Boxer Rising in China.	Joseph Conrad, *Lord Jim*. Anton Chekhov, *Uncle Vanya*.
1901	Death of Queen Victoria: Edward VII becomes King. Negotiations for Anglo-German alliance end without agreement.	Rudyard Kipling, *Kim*.
1902	Treaty of Vereenigung ends Boer War. Triple Alliance between Austria, Germany and Italy renewed for another six years.	Arthur Conan Doyle, *The Hound of the Baskervilles*. Elgar, 'Pomp and Circumstance March No 1'.
1903	King Edward VII visits Paris and French President Loubet visits London – beginning of Entente Cordiale. Wright Brothers' first flight.	Jack London, *The Call of the Wild*. Film: *The Great Train Robbery*.
1905	End of Russo-Japanese War. Revolution in Russia following 'Bloody Sunday'.	E M Forster, *Where Angels Fear to Tread*. Edith Wharton, *House of Mirth*.

YEAR	AGE	THE LIFE AND THE LAND
1908	29	May: AS elected for first time to Bulgarian parliament; he serves as a deputy from 1908 to 1911 and 1913 to 1923.
		Oct: Bulgaria declares complete independence; Ferdinand proclaims himself 'King of the Bulgarians'.
1909	30	Publication of AS's *Politcheski partii ili sŭslovni organisatsii?* (Political parties or estate organisations?), the first collated exposition of agrarian ideas.
1912	33	Oct: First Balkan War begins with joint Bulgarian-Greek-Serbian-Montenegrin attack on Ottoman territory.
1913	34	May: Treaty of London awards Bulgaria considerable gains in Macedonia and Thrace.
		16 Jun: Bulgaria attacks former Greek and Serbian allies; Second Balkan War begins.
		Jul: Defeated Bulgaria signs Treaty of Bucharest, losing most of its previous gains.
		Sep: Treaty of Constantinople returns much of Thrace to Ottoman Empire.
1914	35	Aug: Bulgaria declares neutrality in the European war.
1915	36	Sep: Bulgaria joins Central Powers in attack upon Serbia; Anti-war AS deprived of his seat in parliament and jailed after fiery altercation with King Ferdinand.

YEAR	HISTORY	CULTURE
1908	*The Daily Telegraph* publishes remarks about German hostility towards England made by Kaiser Wilhelm II. Union of South Africa is established.	Kenneth Grahame, *The Wind in the Willows*. Anatole France, *Penguin Island*.
1909	State visits of Edward VII to Berlin and Rome. Kiamil Pasha, grand vizier of Turkey, forced to resign by Turkish nationalists.	H G Wells, *Tono-Bungay*.
1912	The Liner *Titanic* sinks; 1,513 die. Woodrow Wilson is elected US President.	Alfred Adler, *The Nervous Character*. C G Jung, *The Theory of Psychoanalysis*.
1913	US Federal Reserve System is established. Grand Central Station, New York, completed.	D H Lawrence, *Sons and Lovers*. Thomas Mann, *Death in Venice*.
1914	Outbreak of First World War.	James Joyce, *Dubliners*. Film: Charlie Chaplin in *Making a Living*.
1915	First World War: Battles of Neuve Chappelle and Loos. The 'Shells Scandal'. Gallipoli campaign. Germans sink the British liner *Lusitania*, killing 1,198.	Joseph Conrad, *Victory*. John Buchan, *The Thirty-Nine Steps*. Film: *The Birth of a Nation*.

YEAR	AGE	THE LIFE AND THE LAND
1916	37	Sep: Bulgarian forces join Central Powers attack on Romania.
1918	39	Sep: Allied forces break through Bulgarian lines in Macedonia.
		25 Sep: AS released from prison in hope that he will calm discontent in the army; he refuses to join government.
		27–30 Sep: Military rebellion centred upon Radomir. After defeat of the rising AS goes into hiding.
		29 Sep: Defeated Bulgaria signs armistice in Salonica.
		3 Oct: Ferdinand abdicates and is succeeded by his son, King Boris III.
		31 Dec: AS amnestied after Radomir rebellion and enters government as minister for public works.

YEAR	HISTORY	CULTURE
1916	First World War. Western Front: Battle of Verdun, Battle of the Somme. US President Woodrow Wilson is re-elected: issues Peace Note to belligerents. Lloyd George becomes Prime Minister.	Lionel Curtis, *The Commonwealth of Nations.* Film: *Intolerance.*
1918	First World War. Peace Treaty of Brest-Litovsk between Russia and the Central Powers. German Spring offensives on Western Front fail. Romania signs Peace of Bucharest with Germany and Austria-Hungary. Ex-Tsar Nicholas II and family executed. Allied offensives on Western Front have German army in full retreat. Armistice signed between Allies and Germany; German Fleet surrenders. Kaiser Wilhelm II of German abdicates.	Alexander Blok, *The Twelve.* Gerald Manley Hopkins, *Poems.* Luigi Pirandello, *Six Characters in Search of an Author.*

YEAR	AGE	THE LIFE AND THE LAND
1919	40	Publication of AS's *Printsipite na BZNS* (The Principles of the BANU), in which his earlier ideas are developed and refined.
		Jul–Aug: AS made a member of the Bulgarian delegation to Paris to await Allied peace terms.
		7 Oct: AS becomes prime minister of a coalition government.
		19 Oct: Peace terms communicated to Bulgarian delegation which had been summoned back to Paris.
		27 Nov: AS signs the Treaty of Neuilly; no other Bulgarian joins him in doing so.
1920	41	21 May: AS forms a purely agrarian government, the first in Europe.
		Oct: AS sets off on a 100-day tour to Britain, France, Belgium, Czechoslovakia, Poland and Romania.
1923	44	Mar: AS signs the Niš convention undertaking to control Macedonian extremists in Bulgaria.
		9 Jun: Right-wing coup topples the BANU government.
		14 Jun: AS murdered.
1925		Aug: Communist bomb in roof of Sveta Nedelya Cathedral, Sofia, kills over 130 leading Bulgarian public figures and precipitates White terror.

YEAR	HISTORY	CULTURE
1919	Communist Revolt in Berlin. Paris Peace Conference adopts principle of founding League of Nations. Benito Mussolini founds fascist movement in Italy. Peace Treaty of Versailles signed. Irish War of Independence begins. US Senate votes against ratification of Versailles Treaty, leaving the USA outside the League of Nations.	Bauhaus movement founded by Walter Gropius. Thomas Hardy, *Collected Poems*. Film: *The Cabinet of Dr Caligari*.
1920	League of Nations comes into existence. League of Nations headquarters moved to Geneva. Bolsheviks win Russian Civil War. Government of Ireland Act passed.	F Scott Fitzgerald, *This Side of Paradise*. Franz Kafka, *The Country Doctor*.
1923	French and Belgian troops occupy the Ruhr. The USSR formally comes into existence. Adolf Hitler's *coup d'état* (The Beer Hall Putsch) fails.	P G Wodehouse, *The Inimitable Jeeves*. George Gershwin, 'Rhapsody in Blue'.
1925	Pound Sterling returns to the Gold Standard. Hitler reorganises Nazi Party. Locarno Treaty signed in London.	Noel Coward, *Hay Fever*. Virginia Woolf, *Mrs Dalloway*. Film: *Battleship Potemkin*.

YEAR	AGE	THE LIFE AND THE LAND
1931		Oct: One agrarian faction included in coalition government.
1934		19 May: Coup by Zveno organisation, assisted by army officers, removes government and imposes semi-authoritarian system. It suppresses Macedonian extremists.
1935		Jan: May 1934 government removed by a palace coup. King Boris increases his power.
1939		Sep: Bulgaria declares neutrality in the European war.
1941		1 Mar: Bulgaria joins the Axis and soon occupies Macedonia and parts of Thrace.
1943		Widespread popular protests save Jews of pre-1941 Bulgaria from deportation to death camps. 28 Aug: Death of King Boris. Simeon II, a minor, becomes King.

YEAR	HISTORY	CULTURE
1931	National Government formed in Great Britain.	Noel Coward, *Cavalcade.* Film: *Dracula.*
1934	Germany, 'Night of the Long Knives'. After German President Hindenburg dies, role of President and Chancellor are merged and Hitler becomes *Führer.* Japan repudiates Washington treaties of 1922 and 1930.	F Scott Fitzgerald, *Tender Is the Night.* Robert Graves, *I, Claudius.* Films: *David Copperfield.*
1935	Saarland is incorporated into Germany following a plebiscite. League of Nations imposes sanctions against Italy following its invasion of Abyssinia.	Karl Barth, *Credo.* *Brockhaus Encyclopaedia* Films: *The 39 Steps. Top Hat.*
1939	Germans troops enter Prague. Italy invades Albania. German invasion of Poland: Britain and France declare war. Soviets invade Finland.	James Joyce, *Finnegan's Wake.* John Steinbeck, *The Grapes of Wrath.* Films: *Gone with the Wind. The Wizard of Oz.*
1941	Second World War. Germany invades USSR Japan attacks Pearl Harbor.	Bertold Brecht, *Mother Courage and Her Children.* Films: *Citizen Kane. Dumbo.*
1943	Second World War. Germans surrender to Russians at Stalingrad. Italy surrenders unconditionally. Tehran Conference: Churchill, Roosevelt and Stalin meet.	Rogers and Hammerstein, *Oklahoma!* Film: *For Whom the Bell Tolls. Bataan.*

YEAR	AGE	THE LIFE AND THE LAND
1944		Sep: Bulgaria breaks with Germany. Soviet troops enter the country.
		9 Sep: Coup in Sofia establishes a communist-dominated government.
		(to 1947) Steady communist pressure emasculates other political groups.
1947		Feb: Peace treaty signed in Paris between Bulgaria and Allies.
		23 Sep: Execution of popular agrarian leader Nikola Petkov after a grotesque show trial.
		Dec: 'Dimitrov' constitution establishes full communist power in Bulgaria.

YEAR	HISTORY	CULTURE
1944	British and US forces in Italy liberate Rome.	Terrence Rattigan, *The Winslow Boy*.
	D-Day landings in France.	Tennessee Williams, *The Glass Menagerie*.
	Claus von Stauffenberg's bomb at Rastenburg fails to kill Hitler.	Film: *Double Indemnity. Henry V. Meet Me in St Louis.*
	British and US forces in Italy liberate Rome.	
	Free French enter Paris.	
1947	'Truman Doctrine' pledges to support 'free peoples resisting subjugation by armed minorities or outside pressures'.	Anne Frank, *The Diary of Anne Frank*.
		Tennessee Williams, *A Streetcar Named Desire*.
	Indian Independence and Partition.	Films: *Monsieur Verdoux. Black Narcissus.*

Further Reading

Literature on Stamboliĭski in English is very limited. The only English translation of his work of which I am aware is Ĭordan Zarchev and Bogomil Vŭlov (eds), *Selected Works/ Aleksandŭr Stamboliiski* (Sofia: 1981), but this is a slim volume of only 104 pages. There are short studies by Khristo Angelov Khristov, *Aleksandŭr Stamboliiski: his life, ideas and work* (Sofia: 1981) which is only 89 pages long and an 18-page pamphlet by Boris Boev, *Alexander Stamboliski, 1879–1979* (Sofia: 1979). That quality can come with quantity is proved by John D Bell, *Peasants in Power: Alexandŭr Stamboliski and the Bulgarian Agrarian National Union, 1899–1923* (Princeton, New Jersey: 1977), the most important single volume in English on Stamboliĭski and the BANU. There is also much of value in Nisssan Oren, *Revolution Administered: Agrarianism and Communism in Bulgaria* (Baltimore and London: 1973). A highly personal and entertaining, if exaggeratedly self-aggrandising account is to be found in Kosta Todorov, *Balkan Firebrand: the Autobiography of a Rebel, Soldier and Statesman* (Chicago: 1943). An agrarian of a later generation is portrayed in Charles A Moser, *Dimitrov of Bulgaria: A Political Biography of Dr*

Georgi D. Dimitrov (Ottawa, Illinois: 1979). Also of value are John D Bell, 'Alexander Stamboliski and the Theory and Practice of Agrarianism in Bulgaria', in Thomas Butler (ed), *Bulgaria Past and Present* (Columbus, Ohio: 1976) pp 78–90, and two articles by Frederick B Chary: 'Agrarians, Radicals, Socialists and the Bulgarian Peasantry, 1899–1905', in Ivan Volgyes (ed), *The Peasantry of Eastern Europe*, Vol. 1, *Roots of Rural Transformation* (Oxford: 1979) pp 35–56, and 'The Politicization of the Bulgarian Agrarian Popular Union, 1899–1901', in Dimitŭr Kosev (ed), *Bulgaria Past and Present* (Sofia: 1982) pp 249–57. An interesting sociological examination of Bulgarian peasant life in the inter-war years is Irwin T Sanders, *Balkan Village* (Lexington, Kentucky: 1949).

The Bulgarian agrarian movement inevitably features in studies of the communism in Bulgaria, for example in: John D Bell, *The Communist Party of Bulgaria from Blagoev to Zhivkov* (Stanford, California: 1986); Nissan Oren, *Bulgarian Communism: The Road to Power, 1934–1944* (New York: 1971); and Joseph Rothschild, *The Communist Party of Bulgaria: Origins and Development, 1883–1936* (New York: 1959).

Stamboliĭski is not alone in having few biographers in English. There is no recent study of Bulgaria's first prince but a sympathetic portrayal is to be found in Egon Corti, *Alexander of Bulgaria* (London: 1954). After the First World War there were many critical lives of Alexander's successor but a more indulgent view was presented in Stephen Constant, *Foxy Ferdinand, Tsar of Bulgaria* (London: 1979). Ferdinand's son received much more generous treatment from English-language biographers. The best account is Stephane Groueff, *Crown of Thorns: the Reign of King Boris III of Bulgaria, 1918–1943* (Lanham, Maryland, New York, and

London: 1987). Stefan Stambolov attracted an early biography in A Hulme Beaman, *M. Stambuloff* (London: 1895); the most authoritative study in English is Duncan Perry, *Stefan Stambolov and the Emergence of Modern Bulgaria, 1870–1895* (Durham, North Carolina, and London: 1993)

The peace treaty of 1919 has received little scholarly treatment, not least because there were no real negotiations. The title of Petko M Petkov's, *The United States and Bulgaria in World War I* (Boulder, Colorado and New York: 1991) is self-explanatory; the book is based on and includes the text of the diaries of Stefan Panaretov who represented Bulgaria in Washington. The atmosphere of the proceedings is captured in Nadezhda Muir, *Dmitri Stancioff; Patriot and Cosmopolitan, 1864–1940* (London: 1957), and Mari Firkatian, *Diplomats and Dreamers* (Lanham MD: 2008).

Recent histories of Bulgaria since 1878 are R J Crampton, *Bulgaria* (Oxford: 2007) and the same author's *A Concise History of Bulgaria* (2nd edn, Cambridge: 2005), but most detail on the period 1878–1918 is to be found in his *Bulgaria: A History, 1878–1918* (Boulder, Colorado and New York: 1983). For the economic history of Bulgaria there is the excellent John R Lampe, *The Bulgarian Economy in the Twentieth Century* (London: 1986).

The Bulgarian national revival has not been fully treated by western writers but there is a volume by one of Bulgaria's most gifted historians: Nikolai Genchev, *The Bulgarian National Revival Period* (Sofia: 1977). The history of the Bulgarian Church is covered fully only in Bulgarian sources but an indication of how fascinating a subject this is can be found in the excellent Thomas A Meininger, *Ignatiev and the Establishment of the Bulgarian Exarchate, 1864–1872* (Madison, Wisconsin: 1970). An authoritative account of the making of

Bulgaria's first constitution is given in C E Black, *The Establishment of Constitutional Government in Bulgaria* (New Jersey: 1943)

The Macedonian problem caused the spilling of almost as much ink as blood. Much of what has been written is too tendentious to record: objective accounts are to be found in H N Brailsford, *Macedonia, its Races and their Future* (London: 1906); and Duncan Perry, *The Politics of Terror: The Macedonian Revolutionary Movements, 1893–1903* (Durham, North Carolina, and London: 1988). The activities of the Macedonian organisations in Bulgaria and their suppression in 1934 is well documented in Joseph Swire, *Bulgarian Conspiracy* (London: 1939).

The classic diplomatic history of the Balkan wars is Ernst C Helmreich, *The Diplomacy of the Balkan Wars, 1912–1913* (New York: 1969). More recent treatments are R J Crampton, *The Hollow Détente* (London: 1979) and Andrew Rossos, *Russia and the Balkans* (Toronto: 1981). Material on both the Balkan wars and the lead-up to the First World War are to be found in Richard C Hall, *Bulgaria's Road to the First World War* (Boulder, Colorado and New York: 1996). Two recent works by André Gerolymatos treat the Balkan Wars in a wider context: *The Balkan Wars: Myth, Reality and the Eternal Conflict* (Toronto: 2001) and *The Balkan Wars: Conquest, Revolution, and Retribution from the Ottoman Era to the Twentieth Century and Beyond* (New York: 2002). A seminal text on the Balkan Wars was The Carnegie Endowment for International Peace, *Report of the International Commission to Inquire into the Causes and Conduct of the Balkans Wars* (Washington, DC: 1914) which was republished with an introduction by George F Kennan as *The Other Balkan Wars* (Washington, DC: 1993).

Bulgaria in the Second World War is portrayed expertly in Marshall Lee Miller, *Bulgaria during the Second World War* (Stanford, California: 1975); for the important question of policy towards the Jews see the admirable Frederick B Chary, *The Bulgarian Jews and the Final Solution, 1940–1944* (Pittsburg: 1972); Michael Bar-Zohar, *Beyond Hitler's Grasp: the Heroic Rescue of Bulgaria's Jews* (Holbrook, Massachusetts: 1998) embodies more recent research but is appallingly badly written. The communist takeover in Bulgaria is brilliantly analysed in Vesselin Dimitrov, *Stalin's Cold War* (Basingstoke and New York: 2008) and the same author has given an equally good guide to events after the fall of the communists in *Bulgaria; the Uneven Transition* (London and New York: 2001). A superb treatment of the Muslim minority in Bulgaria is Mary Neuburger, *The Orient Within: Muslim Minorities and the Negotiation of Nationhood in Modern Bulgaria* (Ithaca and London: 2004); also of value are K H Karpat (ed), *The Turks of Bulgaria: The History, Culture and Political Fate of a Minority* (Istanbul: 1990) and Bilal N Simsir, *The Turks of Bulgaria (1878–1985)* (London: 1988).

Picture Sources

The author and publishers wish to express their thanks to the following sources of illustrative material and/or permission to reproduce it. They will make proper acknowledgements in future editions in the event that any omissions have occurred.

Stanciov Collection: p xii; Topham Picturepoint: p 72. All other pictures private collections or public domain.

Endpapers

The Signing of Peace in the Hall of Mirrors, Versailles, 28th June 1919 by Sir William Orpen (Bridgeman Art Library)
Front row: Dr Johannes Bell (Germany) signing with Herr Hermann Müller leaning over him
Middle row (seated, left to right): General Tasker H Bliss, Col E M House, Mr Henry White, Mr Robert Lansing, President Woodrow Wilson (United States); M Georges Clemenceau (France); Mr David Lloyd George, Mr Andrew Bonar Law, Mr Arthur J Balfour, Viscount Milner, Mr G N Barnes (Great Britain); Prince Saionji (Japan)
Back row (left to right): M Eleftherios Venizelos (Greece);

Dr Afonso Costa (Portugal); Lord Riddell (British Press);
Sir George E Foster (Canada); M Nikola Pašić (Serbia);
M Stephen Pichon (France); Col Sir Maurice Hankey,
Mr Edwin S Montagu (Great Britain); the Maharajah of
Bikaner (India); Signor Vittorio Emanuele Orlando (Italy);
M Paul Hymans (Belgium); General Louis Botha (South
Africa); Mr W M Hughes (Australia)

Jacket images

(Front): akg Images.

(Back): *Peace Conference at the Quai d'Orsay* by Sir William
Orpen (akg Images).

Left to right (seated): Signor Orlando (Italy); Mr Robert
Lansing, President Woodrow Wilson (United States); M
Georges Clemenceau (France); Mr David Lloyd George, Mr
Andrew Bonar Law, Mr Arthur J Balfour (Great Britain);
Left to right (standing): M Paul Hymans (Belgium); Mr
Eleftherios Venizelos (Greece); The Emir Feisal (The
Hashemite Kingdom); Mr W F Massey (New Zealand);
General Jan Smuts (South Africa); Col E M House (United
States); General Louis Botha (South Africa); Prince Saionji
(Japan); Mr W M Hughes (Australia); Sir Robert Borden
(Canada); Mr G N Barnes (Great Britain); M Ignacy
Paderewski (Poland)

Index

Makers of the Modern World

UK PUBLICATION: November 2008 to December 2010
CLASSIFICATION: Biography/History/
    International Relations
FORMAT: 198 × 128mm
EXTENT: 208pp
ILLUSTRATIONS: 6 photographs plus 4 maps
TERRITORY: world

Chronology of life in context, full index, bibliography innovative layout
with sidebars